Charles Hartshorne and The Existence of God

SUNY Series in Philosophy
Robert C. Neville, Editor

CHARLES HARTSHORNE
AND THE EXISTENCE OF GOD

Donald Wayne Viney

State University of New York Press
ALBANY

Published by
State University of New York Press, Albany

©1985 State University of New York

All rights reserved

Printed in the United States of America

For information, address State University of New York
Press, State University Plaza, Albany, N.Y., 12246

Library of Congress Cataloging in Publication Data

Viney, Donald Wayne.
    Charles Hartshorne and The Existence of God.

    (SUNY series in philosophy)
    Bibliography: p.
    Includes index.
    1. Hartshorne, Charles, 1897–   —Theology.   2. God
—Proof—History of doctrines—20th century.   I. Title.
II. Series.
B945.H354V56   1984   212'.1   83-24269
ISBN 0-87395-907-8
ISBN 0-87395-908-6 (pbk.)

10 9 8 7 6 5 4 3 2 1

For Jenny

Acknowledgements

Approximately 485 words reprinted from *A Natural Theology for our Times* by Charles Hartshorne by permission of The Open Court Publishing Company, La Salle, Illinois, c 1967 by The Open Court Publishing Company.

Approximately 1515 words reprinted from *Creative Synthesis and Philosophic Method* by Charles Hartshorne by permission of The Open Court Publishing Company, La Salle, Illinois, c 1970 by The Open Court Publishing Company.

Contents

Foreword

Dr. Viney has written an excellent account of my treatment of an ancient problem, with special attention to my reasons for believing in God (as I have learned, with the aid of many great writers, to conceive God). With this special emphasis upon reasons for belief, Viney's book can help to correct the impression my work may have made upon some that my chief or only answer to the question, is it rational to believe in God? is the ontological argument. As Viney, I think, shows, this is far from the case.

Viney's account is remarkably accurate, faithful to my meanings. (This does not mean that he agrees with me entirely, or I with him.) His book is well-planned, well-executed, and deftly, lucidly written. It is thoughtful, supporting my six theistic arguments (together constituting a "global" or cumulative argument) with considerations derived partly from my various writings and partly from the general literature and his own reflections. It is critical, looking for "soft spots," but looking also for possible ways to strengthen what my treatment left weak. As a whole, I find his book, with its judicious quotations, a helpful introduction to my philosophical religion or religious philosophy. The first chapter, on the cumulative argument, is a contribution in itself, a result of original research by Viney. Anyone concerned about the reasons for belief should consult this chapter.

I wish to make some remarks about the essay called "Six Theistic Proofs" (pp. 275–97 of my *Creative Synthesis and Philosophic Method*). This essay, frequently quoted from by Viney, appeared first in *The Monist*, 54, No. 2 (April, 1970). Only in these twenty-three pages do I give a complete, though succinct, statement of my reasons for believing in God. The basic scheme, employed in all six "proofs" (I now prefer to call them arguments), is without close precedent, even in my writings. I had, about twenty years before, presented an early version of it to the departmental seminar at the University of Chicago. Rudolf Carnap was present and made a criticism of the first of the six arguments. This led me to reformulate that argument. I withheld publication of the essay for many years, feeling that I had not achieved the clarity I thought possible. Finally, asked to write on the subject for *The Monist*, I arrived at a revision that seemed right. I still think that it does a job that needed to be done and that no one else, including myself, had previously done. Apart from Viney, so far as I have noticed and can recall, little attention has been paid to my new proposal in a language game as old as Plato (*Laws*, X). This suggests that most of my contemporaries assumed they already knew my reasons for belief. If so, this book should show them they were mistaken.

Even Viney, who understands my position, and who takes his formulations of five of the six "proofs" from the essay referred to, does not do so in his discussion of the first or ontological argument. Nor does he emphasize, as much as I do, the uniqueness of the *Monist* or *Creative Synthesis* discussion. I here give the omitted formulation.

A1 Deity cannot be consistently conceived.
A2 Deity can be consistently conceived, equally whether as existent or as nonexistent.
A3 Deity can be consistently conceived, but only as nonexistent, or as an unactualizable or regulative ideal or limiting concept.
T   Deity can be consistently conceived, but only as existent.

The other five arguments have a broadly similar form. (In one case there is an A4.) A stands for atheism, any nontheistic philosophy; T for theism. The idea is to exhaust the a priori mutually exclusive possibilities of affirming or denying the divine existence. If a person can be satisfied to affirm any one of the A forms, then for that person the argument fails. If, as for me, all three are unacceptable, then the argument succeeds, unless the person simply does not know, is a theological agnostic in the strict sense. As Viney neatly shows, an argument in this form can be turned into a standard deduction by prefixing a negation sign to each of the three (or more) A's. Thus if it is false that deity is not conceivable, false that deity is conceivable both as existent and as nonexistent, and false that deity is conceivable only as nonexistent, then it is true that deity is conceivable, but only as existent; and then the atheist contradicts him or her self by claiming to conceive what has been admitted to be inconceivable. A1 could be called positivism (Carnap asserted it), A2 (unqualified) empiricism (John Hick); A3 is less readily named, but is something like Kant's position, and has also affinities with Feuerbach's humanism or Comte's worship of humanity. T is "Anselm's principle" (but not his definition of God).

My preference for not giving the arguments a deductive form is that, as by this time nearly everyone knows, a person who is strongly averse to accepting theism will find a way to disbelieve any premise or combination of premises from which theism is deducible. And this is true for any basic philosophical belief, positive or negative, religious or irreligious. People cannot be coerced by mere logic, unless in pure mathematics. The form I have invented renounces the pretense to settle fundamental questions by deductive logic. The only thing that the proposed form puts pressure on people to do, and that I think constitutes the essential element in rational procedure in metaphysics, is to face the dilemmas, trilemmas, or quatrilemmas that their beliefs or disbeliefs confront them with. (Sometimes there are more than four or five options. As I show in the preceding essay, chapter 13, of the same book, there are exactly nine ways of conceiving the modal status—necessary, contingent, or, in different aspects, both—of God and the world, assuming that both exist.)

As Viney makes clear, I hold that the divine existence is not the only existence that obtains necessarily. If "world" means some form of positive reality distinguishable from God, then it is as true that there must be a world as that there must be God. Ideas of metaphysical generality (if coherently conceived) cannot be uninstantiated. I reject the notion that a decision among options in metaphysics (as I, also Kant and Aristotle, define that word) can be made on empirical grounds. I accept Hume's and Kant's rejection of empirical arguments for theism, and Kant's rejection of empirical arguments against theism. All the reasonable arguments, properly formulated, are—like the ontological argument—reasonings from concepts. (That no concepts apply necessarily to existence is an antitheistic as well as antimetaphysical dogma, not a justified axiom of logic.) Duns Scotus long ago reached this position. My quarrel with him is that I regard his form of theism as either self-inconsistent or meaningless.

I warmly recommend this book and its author.

Charles Hartshorne

Key to Hartshorne References

References to Hartshorne's books occur in brackets throughout the text. The source is cited by an abbreviation of the book title followed by the page number.

OD   *An Outline and Defense of the Argument for the Unity of Being in the Absolute or Divine Good*, unpublished doctoral dissertation, Harvard 1923

BH   *Beyond Humanism: Essays in the Philosophy of Nature.* Gloucester, Mass.: Peter Smith, 1975, originally published in 1937

MVG   *Man's Vision of God and the Logic of Theism.* Chicago: Willet, Clark Co., 1941

DR   *The Divine Relativity: A Social Conception of God.* New Haven: Yale University Press, 1948

RSP   *Reality as Social Process: Studies in Metaphysics and Religion.* Boston: The Beacon Press, 1953

PSG   *Philosophers Speak of God.* With William L. Reese. Chicago: University of Chicago, 1953.

LP   *The Logic of Perfection and Other Essays in Neoclassical Metaphysics.* La Salle, Il.: Open Court, 1962

AD   *Anselm's Discovery.* La Salle, Il.: Open Court, 1965

NT   *A Natural Theology for Our Time.* La Salle, Il.: Open Court, 1967

CS   *Creative Synthesis and Philosophic Method.* La Salle, Il.: Open Court, 1970

WP   *Whitehead's Philosophy: Selected Essays, 1935–1970.* Lincoln: University of Nebraska Press, 1972

AW   *Aquinas to Whitehead: Seven Centuries of Metaphysics of Religion.* Milwaukee: Marquette University Pub., 1976

WV   *Whitehead's View of Reality.* With Creighton Peden. New York: Pilgrim Press, 1981

IO   *Insights and Oversights of Great Thinkers; An Evaluation of Western Philosophy.* Albany, New York: State University of New York Press, 1983

OT   *Omnipotence and Other Theological Mistakes.* Albany, New York: State University of New York Press, 1984.

There have been arguments to prove or disprove a purely absolute being; and others which, if they proved anything, could only establish the existence or nonexistence of a purely relative and contingent God; but what is hard to find (until Schelling or later impossible) is an argument explicitly and clearly bearing on the question whether there is a God both absolute or necessary and (in another aspect) relative or contingent, that is, reflexively transcendent. Such arguments are possible, and only when philosophers have considered them with something of the care they have bestowed upon arguments dealing with a less intelligible conception will it be time to say that the arguments for God's existence have been either validated or invalidated. The question we need to investigate concerns the existence of a being whose nature conforms to the formal structure of the idea: "surpassing itself and all others."

Charles Hartshorne (RSP, 124–125)

Introduction

Charles Hartshorne has long been known for his lively defense of the ontological argument. What few realize, however, is that the ontological argument is not the only reason, or even the most important reason, that Hartshorne is a theist. Hartshorne says,

> If I were asked, "Why do you believe in God?," I would not reply, "Because of the ontological argument." Rather, I would say that it is because of a group of arguments that mutually support one another so that their combined strength is not, as Kant would have it, like that of a chain which is as weak as its weakest link, but like that of a cable whose strength sums the strength of its several fibers.[1]

The nexus of arguments to which Hartshorne refers is called the global argument. Surprisingly, even some careful students of Hartshorne's thought are ignorant of the important role the global argument plays in Hartshorne's theism. David Pailin, for example, criticizes Hartshorne's ontological argument on the grounds that it does not prove the concept of God is coherently conceivable.[2] This is a criticism Hartshorne, time and again, has acknowledged.[3] Hartshorne never took the ontological argument to be a complete proof of theism.

In the twelve years since Hartshorne first explicitly formalized the global argument, not one article, book, or dissertation has dealt with the argument in more than a cursory fashion.[4] Hartshorne admits that he may be partially responsible for the neglect of his argument. The 1970 presentation of the global argument is sketchy and brief.[5] Nevertheless, the present work (see especially Chapter II) proves that the global argument has been part of Hartshorne's philosophy ever since his days at Harvard in the 1920s.

The misunderstanding of Hartshorne's position and the relative neglect of the global argument provide the *raison d'être* of this work. It is also my purpose to highlight the fact that the global argument is a *cumulative case*. The case for God's existence is built on a series of interrelated arguments which support each other at their weakest points.

1

Too many philosophers of religion labor under the assumption that theism stands or falls with the success or failure of a single argument. The global argument is a much needed remedy for this prevalent misconception.

Chapter I discusses the concept of a cumulative case and answers the few objections that have been raised against such an enterprise. Chapter II deals with the history and form of Hartshorne's cumulative case. Chapter III familiarizes the reader with Hartshorne's concept of God. Chapters IV through IX take up the elements of the global argument on an individual basis. Thus, there are discussions of the ontological argument, the design argument, the moral argument and so on. Chapter X attempts to show the interrelations among the elements of the global argument and offers some critical observations of Hartshorne's position.

According to Hartshorne, an entire metaphysical system can be spun from a sufficiently clarified concept of God (CS 39). The global argument, therefore, could be understood as a restatement of some of the major themes of Hartshorne's metaphysics. Understanding this, I often became dizzy contemplating the complexity of the task before me. To keep the work to a manageable length it was often necessary to discuss problems with less thoroughness than they deserve. Nevertheless, it is hoped that this overview of the global argument can serve as a basis for a better understanding of Hartshorne's thought and as an impetus for future dialogue.

When writing on the topic of God's existence and nature it has become customary in contemporary circles to apologize for using masculine pronouns when referring to God. Some writers attempt to circumvent the problem by using both masculine and feminine pronouns alternately or at random.[6] This device, while displaying sensitivity to the problem of sexist language, is rather artificial and confusing. Moreover, it is not really a solution. It performs plastic surgery on the language where something more radical is required. Mary Daly points out that the word God is saturated with male dominated connotations.[7] Although I agree with Daly, her solution to use Goddess seems overly reactionary. I have reluctantly retained God and the use of masculine pronouns for want of better terms.

Rosemary Reuther argues that the sexism of the Christian tradition is intimately related to the dualistic worldview inherited from the Greeks.[8] By assimilating the male/female distinction to the spirit/matter dichotomy, a model for male dominance was written into the very structure of existence. Thus, a first step in overcoming sexism in religion is to rethink the dualistic assumptions inherent in the Greek tradition. One of the hallmarks of process theology is its criticisms of dualism. Thus, it is not surprising to find Daly, in an earlier work, being friendly to Hartshorne's neoclassical metaphysics.[9] What is required is a more thorough examination of the relevance of process theology for woman's experience and of woman's experience for process theology. In time perhaps the male imagery associated with *God* can be transformed to suggest supreme personhood without either masculinity or femininity.

The preparation, development and writing of this book involved persons, only a handful of whom can be named. Charles Hartshorne has my gratitude for reading and critiquing the entire manuscript while it was still in its form as my dissertation. During that time, and despite a lengthy illness of his wife, Professor Hartshorne aided me with prompt replies to my letters and words of encouragement. Working under Professor Hartshorne's guidance has been a rare privilege. I also wish to thank him for contributing the Foreword, without which this book would have remained incomplete.

My debt to Dr. Robert Shahan is probably beyond repayment. By inviting Hartshorne to serve on my doctoral committee he is indirectly responsible for opening the door to a rewarding professional friendship.

Others who have read and criticized the completed work are Professors Tom Boyd, Francis Kovach, Kenneth Merrill and Stewart Umphrey. Each one, more than once, saved me from ambiguity of statement, or in some cases, outright error.

The financial and emotional support of my parents, Wayne and Noni Viney, was indispensable in the making of this book. My father invited me to accompany him on an expense free trip to Harvard University in January 1982. There I read Hartshorne's dissertation and was able to trace the threads of his thought to a time before his professional career began.

Professor J. Clayton Feaver was the first who suggested publishing the manuscript. His faith in the quality of my work has had more of a sustaining influence on my career than he may ever know.

I will always be grateful to Drs. Gary Nowlin and Peter Hutcheson. Through long hours of conversation and lengthy correspondence with these friends, many of my ideas took shape. Jerome Klingaman is to be thanked for his helpful suggestions on some of the revisions of the text.

Others I wish to acknowledge are Susan Taylor, who patiently typed the entire book twice, once as my dissertation and once in its revised format, Gregory Bassham, who gave freely of his time to help make the index, William Eastman, a publisher sensitive to the desires of his author, and Michelle Bakay, the talented artist and good friend whose line drawing of Professor Hartshorne makes this book a work of art, not alone a piece of scholarship.

Finally there is my wife Chris, whose constant faith in my potential was no small factor in the attainment of my professional goals.

I have worked hard trying to remain faithful to the meaning and spirit of Hartshorne's philosophy. If in some instances I have failed I accept full responsibility while trusting the critic to go to Hartshorne's own work to remedy the problem.

Donald Wayne Viney
Norman, Oklahoma
October 1983

I
The Idea of a Cumulative Case

Rational support for theism has traditionally taken the form of offering one or more of the standard proofs of God's existence. The proofs are usually presented as if each one must bear the full weight of the theistic conclusion, much as the center post of a tent must support the entire weight of the canvas. But is there any more reason to believe that theism stands or falls with the success or failure of one argument than there is to believe that a tent must have only one supporting post? Just as more than one post is often needed to support a large tent, more than one argument may be required to justify belief in God. Several arguments, when taken individually, may be weak, but when considered as elements of one cumulative case, may be strong. The aim of this chapter is to explain and defend the idea of a multiple-argument strategy for theism.

Mitchell refers to the combining of several theistic arguments as a cumulative case.[1] He suggests that

> What has been taken to be a series of failures when treated as attempts at purely deductive or inductive argument could well be better understood as contributions to a cumulative case. On this view the theist is urging that traditional Christian theism makes better sense of all the evidence available than does any alternative on offer, and the atheist is contesting the claim.[2]

One need not, as Mitchell does, identify theism with Christian theism in order to understand the point. Since the time of Hume and Kant, philosophers and theologians have become increasingly sceptical of the ability of a single argument to prove God's existence. Such incredulity is perhaps not surprising. For a concept as ambiguous as the concept of God and for a subject as complex as religion, one should hardly expect a single argument to settle major issues. Thus, the assumption that the case for theism must rest with one argument cannot go unchallenged.

5

The various theistic arguments may be considered as elements of one cumulative case. Mitchell notes that

> *Prima facie* the elements of the theistic scheme do tend to reinforce one another in a way that is recognizable both to theists and by their opponents.[3]

In the mouths of its more articulate defenders, theism presents a more or less coherent world-view. The universe is said to depend upon or be part of a greater unseen reality. The cosmological and design arguments for God's existence serve to focus this claim by providing one way of explaining the existence and order of nature. And, it may be, as Kant argued, that if the cosmological argument is sound, some form of the ontological argument must also be sound. It is arguable that the reality upon which all else depends must be a necessary reality, necessarily existing, and therefore implied in the very concept of existence. The claims of some mystics to have been in direct contact with this higher reality reinforce the theist's belief in God. Many varieties of theism also maintain that God is personal and is actively concerned for the welfare of his creatures. Thus, the existence of putative revelations from God tend to support the other elements of the theistic scheme. Add to these considerations the fact that those individuals recognized by the religious community as being specially informed by the spirit of God exhibit rare qualities of courage, moral fortitude, and charity, and the case for theism becomes even stronger.

The critic will be quick to point out that each of the arguments in the theistic scheme is subject to serious criticism. It may be argued, for example, that a call for explanation is legitimate only within the universe and that therefore there is no need to explain the universe itself. Thus, neither the cosmological nor the design argument can be successful explanations of the universe. Or again, the concept of a necessary being as employed in the ontological argument has been called incoherent by some philosophers. The critic could also raise the standard criticisms of the arguments from religious experience or revelation. In short, none of the elements of the theistic scheme is immune from attack. But such criticisms are not to the point. What is at issue is whether the various pieces of evidence used to defend theism buttress each other so as to form a stronger case for theism than any one of them could provide in isolation from the others. The theist can agree with the critic that none of the arguments for the existence of God, when taken individually, justify theism. But he or she may still insist that, when taken collectively, a firm foundation for theism can be established.

Many are the attacks on theism which presuppose that it must be justified by arguments taken singly or not at all. For example, far too much weight has been given to Hume's criticism of the traditional design argument that it does not warrant the inference to an almighty, infinite and wise creator.[4] Hume's criticism is correct. But if the design argument were to prove, or make probable the existence of some sort of intelligence behind the universe, the case for theism would have been strengthened. Even Hume concedes this much. The fact that the design argument does not prove that the designer has all the characteristics of God, as traditionally conceived, is not a good reason for supposing that the argument cannot be useful to the theist in providing justification for his or her position. The same is true, *mutatis mutandis*, of the other theistic arguments.

In offering a cumulative case, the theist is not claiming to have dealt a fatal blow to the nontheist. The theist can consistently acknowledge that there are pieces of evidence that tend to count against his or her position. Mitchell, for example, believes that the existence of apparently useless suffering counts against the existence of a loving God. But he does not believe that the problem of evil constitutes a conclusive refutation of theism.

> . . . the theologian *does* recognize the fact of pain as counting against Christian doctrine. But it is true that he will not allow it—or anything—to count decisively against it . . . [5]

Although the theist may admit that evil is a problem for theism, he or she will insist that, when all else is considered, theism makes more sense of the evidence than any of the available alternatives. Mitchell notes that the theist is not in a unique position. The purely naturalistic metaphysic adopted by the atheist is also subject to probing criticism.

> The atheist, too, is able to appreciate that, for instance, conspicuous sanctity is a phenomenon which tells against his position, just as the existence of apparently gratuitous suffering argues for it.[6]

In this same spirit, Hartshorne has long pointed to what he sees as serious deficiencies in any purely naturalistic world-view.[7] Neither theist nor atheist is in a privileged position with respect to the evidence. Neither position is so firmly established that counter-argument is unavailing. The problem of evil and the problem of sanctity are merely examples to make a more general point: Whatever position one takes, and no matter how reasonable the person believes it to be, there will invariably be counterarguments, recalcitrant facts, and loose ends that do not fall neatly into place.

Recognizing that all world-views have their problems, Hartshorne has suggested that the principle of least paradox be adopted as a rule for evaluating competing world-views. According to this principle,

> . . . no position can be argued for merely on the ground that other positions present paradoxes. One must decide which paradoxes are the really fatal ones, in comparison with those of contending positions. (CS 88).

The principle of least paradox can probably not be spelled out in more definite terms. Exactly how many problems a world-view can have before becoming implausible, unreasonable, or indefensible is partly a subjective matter. This is not surprising in light of how complex metaphysical problems can be. Nevertheless, the value of the principle of least paradox is that it serves as a reminder that one's position need not be invulnerable to be defensible. As long as there is good reason to believe that, on balance, the problems of the opponent's arguments outweigh the problems in one's own, there is a justification for not surrendering.

An important consideration, raised by Mitchell, is that the alternatives to the theistic scheme must have some plausibility to be considered as genuine alternatives.[8] For example, it is no criticism of the argument from religious experience that there are, besides the theistic explanation, other possible explanations of religious experience. These other alleged explanations must be weighed in the balance with the theistic explanation to see which better accounts for the phenomena. We would consider it at best a bad joke if someone were to criticize modern theories of disease on the grounds that it is possible that diseases are caused by evil spirits in the blood. Such an explanation, while possible, is so completely out of tune with the rest of our knowledge and theories about the world that it carries no weight as an explanation. Similarly, it is not sufficient to say that alternatives to theistic explanation are possible. Most theists will concede this point but insist that the theistic scheme best accounts for the phenomena under consideration.

The analogy between theories of disease and religious hypotheses suggests that theism must be an empirical issue. But some theists believe the issue is not empirical. According to Popper, a statement is empirical if it is falsifiable by some conceivable experience. Theists differ, however, about whether the existence of God is an empirical question. For example, Hartshorne says,

> The bare question of divine existence is purely nonempirical. Hence empirical existential proofs in natural theology are bound to be fallacious. (NT 52).

He goes on to say that "All the arguments are just as truly a priori as the ontological." (NT 53). In his treatment of the idea of a cumulative case, Mitchell is not sufficiently careful to distinguish empirical from nonempirical approaches to the theistic question. The same can be said of J. L. Mackie's recent discussion of theistic arguments.[9] Care must be taken, however, not to exclude those who approach the question of God's existence nonempirically. There are nonempirical as well as empirical cumulative cases.

The difference between an empirical and a nonempirical or *a priori* cumulative case is a difference in the *modality of the conclusion* they seek to establish. Most theists would agree that, if God exists, his existence is necessary. But there is profound disagreement about how to interpret the concept of necessary existence. A minimal characterization of a necessary being is a being who was not brought into existence and who cannot be deprived of existence. Such a being would exist eternally, "from everlasting to everlasting." This concept of necessity is called ontological necessity. The disagreement among theists (and atheists for that matter), is whether an ontologically necessary or eternal being could conceivably fail to exist. Just as some philosophers have believed that the world is eternal but might have failed to exist, so some theists believe that God is a necessary being, but it is conceivable that he might not exist. The existence of such a God would be ontologically necessary, but logically contingent. Some philosophers, however, claim that an ontologically necessary being must also be *logically* necessary. We are not concerned here to argue for either position (that comes later, in chapter IV); we are only making a map of the various alternatives. Put simply, God's existence is either logically necessary or logically contingent. A God whose nonexistence is conceivable is logically contingent (although the theist will claim God is ontologically necessary). A God whose nonexistence is inconceivable is logically necessary.

How one views the logical modality of God's existence determines the kind of cumulative case one can give. If God's existence is believed to be logically contingent then the cumulative case is called empirical. If God's existence is believed to be logically necessary then the cumulative case is nonempirical, or *a priori*. Normally, an *a priori* cumulative case will make no appeal to contingent truths. The premises of the arguments in an *a priori* cumulative case are usually necessary truths. There is no contradiction, however, in arguing from a contingent premise to a necessary conclusion. One might believe that God's existence is logically necessary and use an argument from authority to support the belief. To my knowledge, no philosopher who uses an *a priori* cumulative case uses an argument from authority. But there is no contradiction in the idea. Neither is there a contradiction in the idea of using a few necessary truths in an empirical cumulative case. Of course, not *all* of the premises of an empirical cumulative case can be necessary truths; for, from necessary truths only necessary truths can follow. Since an empirical cumulative case attempts to establish a logically contingent conclusion, some of the premises must be logically contingent.

Inevitably, a distinction, such as that between empirical and *a priori* cumulative cases, reveals the biases of the one making the distinction. I happen to believe that all logically contingent propositions are falsifiable by some conceivable experience (whether divine or nondivine), and are thus empirical in the Popperian sense. Needless to say, some would argue that God's existence is a necessary condition of there being any world (and thus any experience), but that God might have failed to exist. According to this view, even though God's existence is logically contingent, no experience could falsify the proposition that God exists. Anyone holding this view will probably be uncomfortable with the idea of calling their cumulative case empirical, since, for them, the conclusion is not an empirical statement. Perhaps "quasiempirical" or "quasi-*a priori*" would be better. Although I will continue to speak only of empirical and *a priori* cumulative cases, this is in no way meant to prejudge the theistic issue. Chapter IV contains an argument for equating logical contingency and empiricality. Until then, no more should be read into the idea of an empirical cumulative case than that it must have a logically contingent proposition as a conclusion.

Historically, few philosophers have self-consciously argued for God's existence using a cumulative case. While it is true that many have offered more than one argument for God's existence, few have been aware of the cumulative nature of their arguments. Three outstanding exceptions to this general trend are Duns Scotus, F. R. Tennant and

David Elton Trueblood.[10] Scotus' argument is perhaps the most sustained effort by any medieval thinker to establish the existence of God. The Scotistic argument employs variations of the ontological, cosmological and teleological arguments. A good case can be made that Scotus considered his own argument to be *a priori*. According to Copleston,

> What Scotus maintains is that all factual propositions relating to finite things are contingent. If true they are contingently true. If therefore these contingently true propositions are used as a basis for proving the existence of God, the conclusion will itself be contingently true. He prefers to argue from the *possibility* of the existence of things. In other words, he tries to show, by means of a complex and lengthy argument, that the existence of God is the ultimate and necessary condition of the possibility of there being any finite thing at all. He assumes of course that while the existence of finite things is not necessary, the possibility of their existence is.[11]

In refusing to argue from the existence of finite beings Scotus seems to want to establish the existence of God on nonempirical grounds. Yet, even if this be denied, it is clear from the structure of his argument that Scotus considered it to be a cumulative case. In separate arguments, Scotus attempts to prove the existence of a being first in the order of efficient causes, a being first in the order of final causes, and a being first in the order of perfection. According to Scotus, all of these first causes are necessary beings. He then offers a proof that there can be only one necessary existent. Finally, Scotus claims that this necessary being, first in the orders of perfection, and final and efficient causation is also infinite. Scotus felt that none of his arguments, taken individually, was sufficient to prove the existence of God. For example, a being which is merely a first efficient cause is not God. Furthermore, without the proof that only one necessary being can exist, Scotus might have succeeded in proving polytheism. Thus, the various arguments require each other; they constitute a cumulative case.

If the Scotistic argument is an example of an *a priori* cumulative case, the works of Tennant and Trueblood represent empirical cumulative cases. In the second volume of his *Philosophical Theology*, Tennant uses epistemological teleological, aesthetic and moral arguments to show that it is more probable than not that God exists. Trueblood uses similar arguments but adds evidence from historical and religious experience. Tennant refers to his argument as a "cumulative theistic argument." Trueblood, discussing the nature of cumulative evidence says, "Since no single line of evidence is ever adequate, our security lies in the phenomenon of convergence."[12]

Unlike Scotus, Tennant and Trueblood are concerned that their arguments be empirical. Says Tennant, "The attributes to be ascribed to God will be such as empirical facts and their sufficient explanation indicate or require."[13] Trueblood indicates his empirical approach by the fact that he adopts Hume's distinction between relations of ideas and matters of fact.[14] The existence or nonexistence of God is understood as a question pertaining to matters of fact. Since, for Hume, no matters of fact are logically necessary, Trueblood must adopt the view that God's existence would be logically contingent. Thus, both Tennant and Trueblood offer empirical cumulative cases. Although their approaches to the theistic question differ, Scotus, Tennant and Trueblood are at one in their belief that theism is to be established by a series of interconnected arguments—in short, a cumulative case.

The outstanding contemporary examples of cumulative cases are those of Swinburne and Hartshorne. Swinburne employs his own versions of the cosmological, design, and moral arguments along with arguments from history, miracles, consciousness, and religious experience.[15] Since Swinburne rejects the idea of an *a priori* argument for theism, it is clear that he takes his own arguments to be empirical.[16] Hartshorne's 'global argument', on the other hand, is clearly a nonempirical cumulative case. Hartshorne repudiates all empirical arguments for the existence of God (*NT* 67). Hartshorne's global argument consists of six proofs, including his famous ontological proof. The cosmological, design, aesthetic, moral and epistemic arguments are all transformed into *a priori* form to complete Hartshorne's cumulative case.

If few have considered the possibility of a cumulative case, it is also true that few have argued against the possibility. Flew, MacIntyre and Scriven are the exceptions to this trend.[17] Their basic objection to the idea of a cumulative case is that several arguments, none of which are valid, cannot possibly add up to a valid argument. MacIntyre says,

> . . . the invalidity of the arguments is such as to preclude the believer from drawing even a limited encouragement from them. One occasionally hears teachers of theology aver that although the proofs do not provide conclusive grounds for belief in God, they are at least pointers, indicators. But a

fallacious argument points nowhere (except to the lack of logical acumen on the part of those who accept it). And three fallacious arguments are no better than one.[18]

Flew makes the same point and labels the putative fallacy the ten-leaky-buckets-tactic. "If one leaky bucket will not hold water that is no reason to think that ten can."[19] Flew's analogy has unfortunate consequences for his own position. Jonathan Barnes has noted that one could carry water in more than one leaky bucket provided their holes do not coincide.[20] Swinburne makes the same point more rigorously:

> An argument from p to r may be invalid; another argument from q to r may be invalid. But if you run the arguments together, you could well get a valid deductive argument; the argument from p and q to r may be valid. The argument from 'all students have long hair' to 'Smith has long hair' is invalid, and so is the argument from 'Smith is a student' to 'Smith has long hair'; but the argument from 'all students have long hair and Smith is a student' to 'Smith has long hair' is valid.[21]

Swinburne goes on to point out that inductive arguments can also be cumulative in nature, as any court of law will show.[22] Flew recognizes this fact but insists there is a distinction between

> . . . the valid principle of the accumulation of evidence, where every item has at least some weight in its own right; and the Ten-leaky-buckets-Tactic, applied to arguments none of which hold water at all.[23]

What Flew has in mind is perhaps best illustrated by an example created by Scriven.

> For something to be evidence for an explanation, it is essential not only that the explanation explain the evidence but that there not be an entirely satisfactory alternative explanation. The fact that North was in Dallas at the time Lee Harvey Oswald was shot is not evidence, even weak evidence, that he did it, since it is perfectly clear that Jack Ruby did it.[24]

Scriven is saying that if there is a perfectly satisfactory explanation of some phenomenon, evidence for alternative explanations is irrelevant since we know that the alternative explanations are false. Since we know that Ruby shot Oswald, there can be no evidence that North is the guilty party. Scriven's point is valid as far as the shooting of Oswald is concerned, but is dubious (at best) when applied to the case for theism. The evidence that Ruby shot Oswald is beyond reasonable doubt. One could hardly say the same concerning the existence of God without begging the question. If we knew that God does not exist then there could be no good evidence that he does exist. But the nonexistence of God is hardly as well established as the fact that Ruby shot Oswald. Theists and their opponents are deeply divided about what is the completely satisfactory explanation of the world. As long as reasonable disagreement remains, the case that God exists and the case that North shot Oswald are simply not analogous. A more appropriate analogy is with the shooting of John F. Kennedy. Reasonable people differ as to how many assassins were involved in Kennedy's death. Since it is not clear how many assassins were involved, there is room for competing explanations. Similarly, there is room for rival explanations of the world. Either God is behind things or not. As in the case with Kennedy's assassination, it is not clear which explanation is correct. Scriven and Flew, of course, have examined many of the main arguments for theism and found them unconvincing. Nevertheless, there are many strong arguments they do not consider (some of the arguments examined in this book are examples). More important, however, is the fact that for every Scriven or Flew there is a Swinburne or Hartshorne who has come to the opposite conclusion. Reasonable people may differ. The ten-leaky-buckets objection is, at best, a *non sequitur* when applied to an issue which, like the existence of God, has no agreed upon solution. The impossibility of a cumulative case for theism, like the impossibility of alternative explanations of Kennedy's assassination, will become apparent only if theism is conclusively refuted.

There are two final objections to the idea of a cumulative case to be considered. Both concern what I have called an *a priori* cumulative case. The first focuses upon the nature of deductive arguments and is suggested by MacIntyre.

> A deductive argument is one in which the conclusion follows from the premises simply because it is already contained in the premises. . . . But now there appears to be something curious about the project of proving the existence of God to

the sceptic or atheist. For if we have a valid deductive argument in which the existence of God is affirmed in the conclusion, then that same existence must also be affirmed in the premises. And anyone who rejects the conclusion will certainly reject at least some of the premises.[25]

There is some ambiguity about what is meant by saying that the conclusion of a valid deductive argument is contained already in the premises (can there be no such thing as synthetic *a priori* propositions?). Moreover, the conclusion of a deductive argument is sometimes not contained in any one of the premises but is contained in the premises distributively. Thus, a person may be inclined to reject the conclusion of the argument but not be inclined to reject any of the premises.[26]

Despite these difficulties there is probably a degree of psychological truth in MacIntyre's argument. Anyone who finds the conclusion of a deductive argument that God exists questionable is also likely to find questionable one or more of the premises used to infer the conclusion. There is a serious point behind the atheist's quip that there can be no sound argument for God's existence since no sound argument has a false conclusion. The rules of logic permit one to deny the conclusion of a valid deductive argument as long as one is willing to deny the truth of one or more of the premises.

If one views the purpose of a proof as a means of intellectually coercing one's opponent into submission, then MacIntyre has raised a formidable barrier to one's project. But there are a variety of ways of understanding proofs for God's existence. Hartshorne agrees with MacIntyre's point but goes on to say:

> But though it is unrealistic to hope that all doubts concerning theism can be removed by deductive argument, it may be quite as unrealistic to suppose that no doubts can be removed. (*NT* 30)

A proof of God's existence may be an important aid in understanding the logic of theism. Hartshorne notes that the theistic proofs may serve as a way of focusing a metaphysical system (MVG 252). The interconnections among fundamental ideas may thus become clearer.

> It may be a good deal easier to see a truth if its logical connections with various propositions, initially not known to be connected with it, are made clear. (*NT* 31).

Furthermore, as Hartshorne notes, a deductive argument establishes "a price for rejecting its conclusion." (*NT* 30). To reject the conclusion of a valid deductive argument it is necessary to reject at least one of the premises. For any single theistic argument, the price paid for rejecting the conclusions may not be too high. Where a cumulative case is concerned, however, there are many premises which must be rejected to maintain the nontheistic position. The nontheist may, on examination of the arguments, judge the price of holding his or her ground too dear to pay. The same thing, in reverse, could happen to the theist. The point, however, is that deductive arguments, especially as elements of a cumulative case, need not be considered superfluous to the defense of theism.

Another objection to the idea of a nonempirical cumulative case runs as follows: It is clear how, in empirical matters, an accumulation of evidence may be necessary to settle an issue. But if the existence of God is a nonempirical question, why should more than one argument be necessary? Would not one *a priori* argument suffice to settle the issue?[27]

This argument can be read two ways. On the first interpretation, the question is why more than one argument for God's existence should be necessary if it is self-evident that God does (or does not) exist. This, however, involves a confusion between necessity and self-evidence. As Plantinga notes, " . . . not all necessary propositions are self-evident."[28] Goldbach's Conjecture and Fermat's Last Theorem are either necessarily true or necessarily false but neither is self-evidently true or false. As noted above, offering a variety of proofs may serve to bring a metaphysical system into sharper focus, thereby facilitating a surer evaluation.

On the second reading, the argument questions the necessity of more than one argument in nonempirical questions. To meet this objection it is sufficient to point out that nonempirical questions often require more than one argument. It is not uncommon for a mathematical proof to involve many subproofs. Furthermore, the more complex the problem, the more likely a series of arguments will be needed to settle the issue. The metaphysical question of God's existence has shown itself to be as complicated as any mathematical or philosophical problem is likely to be. It is therefore natural to expect that something like a cumulative case is most appropriate for confronting the issue.

Most philosophers would agree with William James when he says that

> The arguments for God's existence have stood for hundreds of years with the waves of unbelieving criticism breaking against them, never totally discrediting them in the ears of the faithful, but on the whole slowly and surely washing out the mortar from between their joints.[29]

The waves of unbelieving criticism of which James speaks have, for the most part, washed only against islands of theistic belief—that is to say, individual arguments for God's existence. But there remain vast and unexplored continents that hold a good deal of promise for the justification of theism. A few theists have seen their way to use the resources of a cumulative case. So far, critics have failed to discredit their enterprise. What remains is the difficult task of examining the complexities of individual attempts to construct a cumulative case—untangling premises from conclusions, assessing the validity of inferences, and probing the depths of argument for suggestions to further inquiry. Let us, then, turn to Hartshorne's *a priori* cumulative case, the global argument.

II

Hartshorne's Cumulative Case: The Global Argument From 1923 to 1970

For a proper understanding of Hartshorne's global argument three pre-
liminaries are necessary, (1) to trace the history of the global argument
in Hartshorne's writings, (2) to see the form in which the argument
is presented, and, (3) to understand Hartshorne's form of theism. The
next chapter will cover the third point, that is, neoclassical theism.
The purpose of this chapter is to cover points (1) and (2). We begin
by sketching the history of the global argument. Discussion then turns
to the form in which Hartshorne presents the argument. Two factors
emerge as important, (a) the division of the global argument between
theoretical and normative proofs, and (b) the relations between the
various elements of the global argument; or more specifically, how or
in what sense the proofs are said to support one another.

Hartshorne wrote his dissertation at Harvard in 1923. The dissertation is, arguably, the first presentation of the global argument. As
William Sessions says, "In an important sense, the whole dissertation
is a single ramified argument for God's existence."[1] Eight arguments
are employed to demonstrate what Hartshorne refers to variously as
Teleological Monism or Personalistic Monism. The position is monistic in the sense that there is one "ultimate and uncompounded Principle or Reality."[2] The position is teleological or personalistic in the
sense that the relation of the many to the one is that of valued to
valuer.[3]

It is not clear that Teleological Monism is identical to neoclassical
theism. Sessions argues that the dissertation has no clear concept of
a di-polar God.[4] There is some truth to what Sessions says. But we
must insist that, however inadequately expressed, Hartshorne's inten-
tions point clearly in the direction of neoclassical theism. The dissertation's answer to the problem of evil substantiates this claim. Evil
is said to be the inevitable result of there being a multiplicity of decision

19

makers. The idea of a power with absolute control over all other individuals is said to be contradictory (*OD* 251). The consequence of
this view is that not everything that happens in the world is for the
best (*OD* 252). Hartshorne's theodicy has not changed to the present
day. But this theodicy is available only to someone who adopts a
position which, if not identical to, is very similar to neoclassical theism.
Closely related to these considerations is the fact that Hartshorne
rejected the idea of the actualization of all possible goods. "We do not
argue for a perfect amount of good—but for a perfect *quality* of goodness
or power." (*OD* 279–280). This echoes the notion of a changing God
in his later work. If not explicitly neoclassical, the dissertation was at
least headed in that direction.

The dissertation's eight arguments for Teleological Monism are taken
from the categories of Being, Individuality, Quality, Relation, Space
and Time, Knowledge, Value, and Perfection (*OD* 83). Only the
arguments from knowledge and perfection survive in anything like
their present form in the global argument of *Creative Synthesis*. The
argument from the category of knowledge is an early statement of the
epistemic argument while the argument from the category of perfection
is Hartshorne's earliest version of the ontological argument. Although
Hartshorne's later philosophy contains an argument from the concept
of Being (the cosmological proof), it is different from the argument
from the category of Being in the dissertation. As Sessions notes, the
dissertation's argument from Being is found nowhere in Hartshorne's
later writings.[5] Elements of the other arguments are found scattered
throughout Hartshorne's work. But none of these arguments—from
Individuality, Quality, Relation, Space and Time, or Value—constitute part of the global argument of *Creative Synthesis*. For this reason
it may seem strange to call the dissertation an early version of the
global argument. The identification is, however, justified if we remember that there is a certain arbitrariness about which proofs are to
compose the one global argument.

> There are as many arguments for God as there are conceptions
> of absolute generality. . . . Since these conceptions are more
> or less arbitrarily divisible into aspects or nuances, there is no
> one final list of arguments. (*MVG* 251).

We conclude that the dissertation is best viewed as an early version
of the global argument.

Man's Vision of God (1941) contains a discussion of the idea of
employing a multiplicity of arguments for God's existence but does

not explicitly carry out the task (MVG 251–252). The ontological argument and a version of the cosmological argument are, however, treated at length. The term "global argument" is first used in A Natural Theology for Our Time (1967). In this work, the global argument is "an argument from the rational necessity of religious experience and of God as its adequate referent." (NT 45). Although treated separately, the global argument is said to "sum up" the other theistic proofs (NT 45). The only other proofs discussed at any length in Natural Theology are the ontological, design and moral arguments.

The form finally taken by the global argument in Creative Synthesis (1970) is first suggested in Philosophers Speak of God (1953). In the 1953 work it is suggested that arguments for God's existence be divided into three, corresponding to ethics, aesthetics and epistemology, and three corresponding to the traditional triad of proofs, the ontological, design, and cosmological (PSG 24–25). These are precisely the arguments of Creative Synthesis. This brings us to our next topic of discussion, the form of the global argument.

The global argument is composed of six arguments. Rather than presenting each argument as a set of premises leading to the theistic conclusion, Hartshorne prefers to list each argument as a series of alternatives, the last of which is neoclassical theism. In chapter VI (on the design argument) I have transposed Hartshorne's argument to illustrate how it looks in more traditional form. The advantage of presenting the arguments as a series of alternatives is that it highlights the options among which one must choose in order to reject neoclassical theism. Hartshorne's mode of presentation is a much needed reminder that atheism is not, as some have supposed, without ontological implications. One pays a price for rejecting theism. Needless to say, with each argument, Hartshorne finds the price too high to pay. This is not to say that he thinks neoclassical theism is without its problems. He simply finds more problems (paradoxes, contradictions, etc.) in other positions than in the neoclassical alternative.

It should be noted that in each of the arguments, it is the neoclassical variety of theism which is the desired conclusion (CS 296). This is an important point insofar as it absolves Hartshorne of the charge of begging the question against other forms of theism. In the cosmological argument, for example, the second alternative, which says that everything that exists is contingent, is compatible with many forms of theism. As noted in the previous chapter, many theists believe that God's existence is logically contingent. Hartshorne disagrees. But this is just to say that not all of Hartshorne's philosophical opponents are atheists.

Some forms of theism share assumptions with atheism. It is these assumptions which Hartshorne argues are mistaken.

We have already noted that the proofs in the global argument are
divided into two groups, the theoretical and the normative. Theoretical arguments are well entrenched in the collective consciousness
of philosophers. That is to say, even if one denies that any of the
theistic arguments work, one is still likely to have no serious difficulty
with the idea that, if God's existence could be proved by reason, the
proof would look something like one of the traditional arguments,
namely, the ontological, cosmological or design.

Philosophers are more suspicious of normative arguments, that is,
arguments which attempt to demonstrate or make probable an existential assertion from normative or valuational considerations. Even
Kant, who gave so much importance to practical reason, denied the
possibility of proving the divine existence from the requirements of
rational action. For Kant, God's existence is merely a postulate of
practical reason. The Kantian position is not without its plausibility.
Should one not guard against the temptation to make value claims
the foundations of one's ontology? Hume warned against deriving an
ought from an is. Is it not equally illegitimate to go *from* ought *to* is?

Hartshorne defends the idea of a normative argument by distinguishing those considerations of value linked only to contingencies,
and those linked to necessities. There is no logical bridge between "X
is something good" and "X exists" where X is something which is
contingent and therefore might have failed to be. If this were not true,
no one would ever go hungry. But if X is something that could not
fail to be, the situation is different. One must distinguish the merely
useful, or what is good for some purposes only, from the *indispensable*,
or what is required for the fulfillment of any purpose whatever.

> It is idle to complain of wishful thinking if the idea is required
> for any wish fulfillment whatever. It is wishful to think that
> one can ride because one would like a horse, but this is rele-
> vant only because there are other wishes which can be satis-
> fied without a horse. For the sake of these other wishes one
> acknowledges the facts. But honestly facing facts cannot have
> value if there is no value. And the theistic question is how
> can there be *any* value, *any* meaning, *any* significance.[6]

Tillich was fond of denying that God is one being among others.
Hartshorne would approve of this but add that God is not one good

among other goods. The point is that, according to the theist, if God does not exist, then there is nothing which could take his place. There would be a "hole" in reality which no finite good could fill. Thus, if there is, in human life, a need for God, then either God exists or philosophy must abandon any hope of making sense of the universe. Barring a retreat into irrationalism, the task of the critic is *not* to try to show how the absence of God's goodness might be compensated by other values; rather, it is to show that nondivine values are all that reasonably *could be* required for human life.

We come now to the second question concerning the form of the global argument. If the global argument is to be a cumulative case, then the various arguments must somehow form a network in which each argument supports and is supported by other arguments. This is not to say that the arguments cannot function independently of one another. But, when combined into the one global argument, they are said to make a more persuasive case for neoclassical theism.

In the dissertation, the arguments are characterized as "independent yet cumulative." (*OD* 87). The arguments are independent in the sense that each is, according to Hartshorne, sufficient to reach the position he calls Teleological Monism (*OD* 88). But the arguments are also, in an important sense, cumulative.

> In the series of categories which follows [i.e., the arguments] the order is in general intended to be such that each category should render more explicit than the previous ones, its own ultimate character as an aspect of Being, hence also should throw the nature of the latter into a clearer light and aid in the interpretation of the previous categories as in their own way likewise functions of the One. (*OD* 83).

The first category discussed in the dissertation is the highly abstract concept of Being. With each argument this abstract outline is filled in by the more concrete "details" provided by the other categories. As Hartshorne says,

> . . . There is a cumulative development in that each [argument] shows itself capable of incorporating the preceding as a more abstract or relatively blind expression of the same truth, and in that the conclusion in each case directly necessitated tends to become, as already indicated, more and more concrete—or, on the advocated view of concreteness more and more explicitly and richly in terms of value. (*OD* 88)

Thus, through the progression of arguments there is a progression from the abstract to the concrete.

Hartshorne's later statements on the interrelations of the arguments modify, if not completely overhaul, the ideas of the dissertation. How far Hartshorne has changed his mind depends on how the concepts of abstractness and concreteness are understood as they are used in the dissertation. If abstractness and concreteness are understood in the sense which Hartshorne finally came to give these terms, then there can be no movement from the abstract to the concrete in a series of metaphysical arguments. None of the arguments of *Creative Synthesis* claim to prove anything but something highly abstract. Hartshorne distinguishes between God's existence and his actuality. The fact, if it is a fact, that God exists, tells nothing about the way in which the existence is actualized. Just as I may exist whether as reading a book or as listening to a symphony, so God exists no matter what concrete details we may specify (the difference being that my existence, unlike God's, is subject to death). The distinction between existence and actuality is explained more fully in the next chapter. Suffice it to say that in Hartshorne's post-dissertation philosophy, existence is abstract while actuality is concrete. But the only thing that any of the elements of the global argument can prove is God's existence, and this is the abstract aspect of God.[7]

Rather than read a total shift in Hartshorne's position, I prefer to interpret the statements of the dissertation as saying not that the arguments become progressively more concrete in the sense Hartshorne later gives this term, but that the progression of arguments makes more and more explicit the implications of theism. As already noted, Hartshorne believes that "each category should render *more explicit* than the previous ones, its own ultimate character as an aspect of Being . . . " (OD 83), [emphasis mine]. This interpretation fits best with what Hartshorne says eighteen years later in *Man's Vision of God*.

> The only value of a multiplicity of arguments is that it diminishes the probability that we have overlooked fallacies in the reasoning, somewhat as performing a mathematical operation by several methods helps to insure that no blunder has been committed . . . (MVG 252).

It may be that, at the time of the dissertation, Hartshorne believed not only that his arguments made the implications of theism more explicit but that they were also able to render more and more concrete conclusions. If he actually held the latter view, it is a position he has since abandoned. But he has not backed away from the idea that a variety of arguments can serve to make the implications of theism more explicit.

Hartshorne's view has also expanded in his acknowledgement that each of the proofs has its weak points. The arguments may, then, serve to buttress each other at their weakest points. For example, Hartshorne believes that the weakest premise of the ontological argument is that it is possible that God exists. The other arguments attempt to show that the concept of God is implied in such fundamental notions as cosmic order, knowledge and beauty. If these ideas are indispensable for a proper understanding of the world and if they imply the concept of God, then it is possible that God exists. The ontological proof supports the others by emphasizing their *a priori* nature. This is a topic to be discussed more extensively in chapter IV.

Besides the relation between the ontological argument and the other proofs, there are others which Hartshorne does not mention. Throughout the course of our discussion I shall highlight these relations. One general comment, however, is in order. Since each of the proofs begins from a different categorical concept, each casts its own unique light on one of the divine attributes. As has been clear from the time of the dissertation, the ontological argument, in a manner, sums up the others by arguing from the concept of a perfect being. A perfect being is one lacking no perfection it could conceivably possess. The other arguments make these perfections explicit. The cosmological argument emphasizes God's necessary existence; the design argument emphasizes God's eminent power; the epistemic argument reasons to an omniscient being; and the moral and aesthetic arguments, in their ways, shed light on God's goodness and beauty. Thus, each of the arguments contributes something to the case for theism.

The history and the form of the global argument should now be sufficiently clear that we can move on to a discussion of Hartshorne's neoclassical theism. We shall then be in a position to look at the elements of the global argument on an individual basis.

III
Neoclassical Theism

Some of Hartshorne's most important contributions to philosophical theology are in his discussions of the idea of God. For more traditional concepts of God, Hartshorne substitutes a dipolar God. Since the global argument is an attempt to establish the existence of the dipolar God, it is important to know precisely what the dipolar God is. Our purpose here is not to argue for the coherence of Hartshorne's brand of theism (although some questions of coherence will arise). Indeed, a major function of the global argument is to deal with the coherence question. We wish only to indicate what Hartshorne means by the term 'God'. Hartshorne refers to his metaphysics of God as "neoclassical." Part, at least, of the reason for this is that there is a continuity between classical and neoclassical concepts of God. Nevertheless, the deficiencies Hartshorne finds in traditional theisms dictate that the concept of God be revised. The purpose of neoclassicism is to overcome the inadequacies and contradictions of classical theism while incorporating its insights. In this chapter we will indicate some of the main deficiencies Hartshorne finds in traditional concepts of deity and show how the dipolar concept of God is designed to overcome these problems.

There are almost as many concepts of God to be found in the history of philosophy as there are philosophers. Hartshorne has done much to clarify the logically possible varieties of theism.[1] One concept of God, however, is distinguished by its popularity among some of the greatest philosophers in the western world. This is what is called classical theism. Classical theism in various forms was espoused by such notable philosophers as Augustine, Anselm, Aquinas, Duns Scotus, Leibniz, Descartes, and Kant. There are, of course, important differences among these philosophers. But there is a common core to their theisms which Hartshorne questions. In order to clarify and evaluate Hartshorne's criticisms, it is important to review some of the major guiding constructs of classical theism.

The heart of classical theism is the denial of potentiality in the supreme being. God is *actus purus*, pure act. Aquinas contends, " . . .

27

God has no admixture of potency but is pure act."[2] There are several reasons for this view of God. The cosmological argument, at least as it is developed by Aquinas, relies on the principle that "the reduction of potentiality to act requires a principle which is itself act . . . "[3] From the fact that things in the world change, that is, proceed from potentiality to act, Aquinas reasons that there is at work a principle which is itself act. This is called God.

Another way to approach the doctrine of God as pure act is to consider the definition of God as the most perfect being. God, as the most perfect being, could lack no perfection. But, were there any potency in God there would be some perfection which he lacked. Thus, God must be a being without potency. It directly follows from the lack of potency in God that God cannot change because change requires potency. God is therefore immutable. The concept of God's immutability also implies that God does not exist in time. He is eternal. Furthermore, since in "every composite there must be act and potency"[4] God must be absolutely simple, having no composition or parts. God is therefore immutable, eternal and simple.

Classical theism also involves the belief that God created the world *ex nihilo*, which is to say, that, in creating the world, he did not rely on any pre-existing material (as does Plato's demiurge). God is also said to be omnipotent, omniscient and perfectly good. Omnipotence, or perfect power, is the ability to bring about any state of affairs, the description of which is not self-contradictory. Omniscience refers to God's knowledge which encompasses past, present and future. This classical interpretation of omniscience follows from God's atemporality mentioned above. God does not anticipate the future, rather, future singulars (and past ones) are eternally present to God's mind. God is also said to be good in the sense of being just and merciful. Not all classical theorists agree about how we come to know these various things about God. Duns Scotus, for example, denied the possibility of a philosophical knowledge of God's omnipotence.[5] Kant went so far as to deny the possibility of any theoretical knowledge of God. Nevertheless, all agree on what they *mean* by the word 'God'. And this is what is important for our purposes.

Hartshorne's attack on classical theism employs both religious and philosophical objections. We are primarily concerned with theism as a philosophical problem. But a brief mention of the religious objections may help clarify Hartshorne's philosophical standpoint. One of the assumptions on which classical theism rests is that dependence is an imperfection. A God who, in any way, was dependent on something outside of himself, was thought to be less than perfect. This is part of the reason for the doctrine of creation *ex nihilo*. God is, as it were, self-contained. Hartshorne questions this view. If we look to common experience for analogies there is, says Hartshorne, an admirable and an imperfect form of dependence. The person who is totally unmoved by the suffering of others is considered something less than human. Those who are capable of sympathetic participation in the feelings of others, on the other hand, are more worthy of respect and admiration. Asks Hartshorne, suppose a man says,

> I can be equally happy and serene and joyous regardless of how men and women suffer around me. Shall we admire this alleged independence? I think not. Why should we admire it when it is alleged of God? (*DR* 44).

Dependence is not always a defect. Therefore, Hartshorne believes in a God who is influenced by, and thus in a sense, dependent on the world. Furthermore, if God is, in some aspect dependent, then the idea of serving God makes sense. If God were in no way dependent on the world then it seems there would be no sense in which we could serve God or add to his glory. The Jesuit motto, *ad majorum Dei gloriam* takes on added meaning for a dependent God.

The sense in which God is independent, according to Hartshorne, is in his resolve always to do what is best.

> There *is* an admirable independence, but it is independence in basic ethical purpose, not in specific concrete experience and happiness. (*DR* 45).

When scripture teaches that God does not change it is not speaking of immutability in the classical theist's sense, rather it has to do with God's promises to his people.[6] Putting it simply, God does not go back on his word. Hartshorne attempts to weave the positive notions of dependence and independence into a coherent concept of God. For further clarification of this concept, let us consider some of the philosophical objections to classical theism.

According to Hartshorne, the exclusion of any change in God results in several paradoxes. One paradox has to do with God's omniscience. Since, in God, there is no potentiality, God's knowledge of the world is eternal. Although the world changes, God's knowledge of the world does not change. But there is a problem with such an assertion. Hartshorne asks,

. . . how can what is not eternally actualized be eternally known? The datum of knowledge is essential to that knowledge, and hence an eternally known datum, being integral to the eternal, must be as eternal as the knowledge of it. (CS 166).

The argument can be expressed in the form of a dilemma. Perfect knowledge conforms perfectly to its object. Now, temporal events are either eternal or they are not. If they are eternal they are not really temporal events. On the other hand, if the events are not eternal then perfect knowledge could not know them eternally.

One way to attempt to escape from the dilemma is to argue that the qualities of the thing known do not necessarily transfer to the knowledge. I may know something ugly without my knowledge itself being ugly. Similarly, God may know temporal events without his knowledge itself being temporal. All that is necessary for God's eternal knowledge of events in time is that those events be *eternally present as occurring in time* to God's mind. Much as all of the points on the circumference of a circle are equidistant from the center, so God is equally present at each moment in time.[7]

This answer fails to meet the objection. The problem of the relation between omniscience (classically understood) and time does not arise from *assuming* that the knowledge of a thing necessarily has the qualities of the thing known. The argument attempts to establish that the knowledge of temporal things must itself be temporal. This is not because knowledge of a thing and thing known necessarily have the same qualities. Rather, it is because one destroys the very nature of a temporal event by thinking it could be known eternally. If something is to be known from all eternity, it must be present from all eternity. But temporal events are not present from all eternity—they are not eternal. Thus, knowledge of them cannot be eternal. The analogy with the circle is also suspect. For future temporal events (some of the points of the circumference) are either actual or possible. If they are actual then they are not future. If they are possible then God must know them *as* possible. True, God must be considered as being fully present at each moment. Here classical theism is correct. But it may be that God is at future moments only as they cease to be future, that is, as they become present.

Hartshorne's position is that God knows future contingencies only as possibilities. It is no objection to this view that God, having perfect knowledge, must know all times, past and future. Hartshorne denies that there are, or could be, any such things as future actualities. There are only future possibilities. Thus, it is no limit on God's knowledge that he knows the future only as possible. Hartshorne asks,

> Is it not the essence of the future that it consists of what may or may not exist, that is, of what is unsettled, indefinite, undecided? If so, then God, who knows all things as they are, will know future events only in their character as indefinite, or more or less problematic, nebulous, incomplete as to details. (*RSP* 158).

Fausto Socinus in the sixteenth century and Jules Lequier in the nineteenth, anticipated Hartshorne's defense of the idea that God can know future contingencies only as possibilities. (*PSG* 226, 229).

The classical theist's justification for thinking God surveys all moments, past, present and future is that God is the supreme cause and the world is the effect. If as Aquinas says, "an effect can be preknown in its cause even before it exists"[8] then God's knowledge of himself as cause entails God's knowledge of the world as effect. Thus, the classical notion of omniscience follows from the ideas of God's self-knowledge and God as creator.

Hartshorne is as quick to reject the classical conception of omnipotence as he is to reject its notion of omniscience. In the first place, Hartshorne's metaphysics is indeterministic. Thus, the cause of a thing need be no more than a necessary condition—not a sufficient condition—for the occurrence of an effect.

> . . . to know a cause adequately is indeed to know its *possible* results. However, causes never imply any precise actual results, but only a range of possible ones. Thus, God, merely in knowing his eternal essence, would know "possible worlds" so far as these are eternally implied by the essence; but he would not thereby know the actual world. Causes always leave results somewhat open for further decision. (*AW* 11).

The classical theist's claim that every event is caused and that a perfect knowledge of a cause entails a perfect knowledge of which effect will occur is tantamount to a denial of indeterminism.

Classical theists are invariably deterministic; more specifically, they are theological determinists—God is, as it were, 'omniresponsible' for all that occurs. The question of how creaturely freedom is possible if

God determines all that occurs is difficult, but a variety of ingenious responses have been developed.[9] All of the answers are species of compatibilism, the doctrine that freedom and determinism are not incompatible. There is, however, a dilemma concerning the problem of moral evil that none seem to have escaped. The most plausible reply to the problem of moral evil is the freewill defense: it is not God, but the free decisions of his creatures which accounts for much of the evil in the world. The problem is that the theological determinist cannot use the freewill defense. For it seems that God could have created a world with less moral evil while in no way infringing upon the freedom of his creatures. Even if it is true that creaturely decisions are the cause of moral evil, it follows from the concept of God's omnipotence that he could have created a world in which there was less moral evil than actually exists, or none at all! Leibniz apparently saw this problem and deduced the momentous conclusion that this is the best of all possible worlds. Voltaire's satire of the Leibnizian solution is unparalleled for its clarity of vision. Few classical theists would be willing to use Leibniz's theodicy. Thus, the classical theist is faced with the problem of moral evil without being able to use the most plausible answer to that problem.

Hartshorne's answer is to abandon the idea of theological determinism in favor of a metaphysics in which each individual has some capacity for self-creation. Although God contributes to the character of each individual, he is not wholly responsible for what an individual becomes. Thus,

> In the cosmic drama every actor no matter how humble, contributes to the play something left undetermined by the playwright. (CS 239).

We are co-creators of the world with God. It follows from this notion of "universal creativity" that the classical concept of omnipotence is erroneous. Hartshorne says,

> [God] is not 'omnipotent' in the Thomistic sense [of having] the power effectively to choose that any possible world, no matter which, shall be actual. (CS 242).

God does not, and logically could not, unilaterally decide which world will be actual; which world is actual is partly determined by beings other than God.

It has been objected that Hartshorne's God is limited, and thus not religiously adequate. Madden and Hare refer to Hartshorne's philosophy of God as 'quasi-theism' to indicate their belief that the neoclassical concept of God is less robust than the classical concept.[10] But just as omniscience does not entail a knowledge of future actualities, so omnipotence does not entail the ability to bring about any conceivable state of affairs. Hartshorne agrees with Whitehead that the divine method of world control is persuasion. "'Persuasion' is the ultimate power; not even God can simply coerce." (CS 239–240). God's power is exerted on individuals and according to Hartshorne,

> Individuals (not alone human individuals) must in some degree
> be self-managed, agents acting to some extent on their own,
> or they are not individuals, concrete units of reality. (CS 30).

If coercion is the ability of a cause to produce an effect, such that the effect is totally determined in all of its details, then an individual cannot be coerced without ceasing to be an individual. Hartshorne says,

> . . . if power means capacity to *guarantee* a particular fully
> specified form of actualization, either for oneself or for another,
> then according to this philosophy there can be no such power.
> It is nonsense or contradiction.[11]

Hartshorne is not denying that the concept of coercion has applicability. In one place he distinguishes the abstract aspects of a decision from the process of deciding. A person who is hypnotized may be told to open a window. But Hartshorne notes,

> Merely "opening the window" is not a concrete act. The
> concrete action includes just how the window is opened, just
> how far, at what split second, with what rationalizing
> explanations (if not to others at least to the person himself),
> with what feeling tone and sense of purpose, duty, or guilt.[12]

The hypnotist may be able to cause the person to open the window. But this is an abstract feature of the concrete process of decision. The person hypnotized remains an individual precisely insofar as he is responsible for some aspects of the decision. Coercion then, at most, refers to some abstract features of a decision. Insofar as God is responsible for the abstract features of creaturely decision he has coercive power. What Hartshorne denies is that anyone, including God, could determine another individual's decision in such a way that no details of the decision were left for the individual's own choosing.[13]

The clearest (but not the only) example of God's persuasive power, in Hartshorne's view, is the regularities in nature—natural laws.

> God decides upon the basic outlines of creaturely actions, the guaranteed limits within which freedom is to operate.[14]

The function of God is not to guarantee that the 'best of all possible worlds' becomes actual. Rather, "The ideal rule sets those limits outside which freedom would involve greater risks than opportunities." (LP 231). Given the reality of individual freedom, any world will contain the possibility for evil. "Risk and opportunity are nonidentical twins having the same root, freedom."[15] Furthermore, since God's power is persuasive, not coercive, natural laws do not describe exact regularities, rather they are statistical. Although no "creature has decided what these laws shall be,"[16] the laws are not exactly conformed to. Individual creaturely decisions

> cannot completely fit such a plan for then they would not be self-determined; or, to put it better, the plan cannot be completely definite and detailed. (WV 23).

Once again we may refer to the distinction between abstract aspect and concrete decision. Natural laws are, at best, an abstract aspect of the behavior of individuals. They provide the broad outlines in terms of which freedom occurs.

If Hartshorne is correct then the natural laws that govern the universe provide the maximal opportunity for good and the minimal risk of evil that is consonant with creaturely freedom. Some philosophers are disinclined to see natural laws in such a favorable light. For example, John Roth, himself a theist, argues that we must reckon with God-as-economist and ask how costeffective God's decisions are. Roth's conclusion is that "we have more power, more freedom, than is good for us."[17] J. L. Mackie reaches a similar conclusion when he says that in knowingly accepting the risk of human wickedness, God would "be open to a charge of gross negligence or recklessness."[18] Hartshorne's unwillingness to accept these views is grounded more in his belief that God's existence can be proved than in any attempt to judge the cost-effectiveness of natural laws by weighing iniquity against saintliness.

> Can it be proved that the opportunities did not justify the
> risks as we now see them? If I believed that I would conclude
> that God will prevent the worst form of nuclear catastrophe
> or that in some way the risks are less than they appear to be.
> For I have more faith in the reasons for belief in God than in
> our ability to estimate the relative values involved in the
> laws of natures, the planetary past, and the chances for the
> human future. (*IO* 336).

Thus, for a complete reply to Roth and Mackie we must await the full
exposition of the global argument.[19]

In the discussion thus far, a general trend is evident. In place of
the classical concept of God as pure act, Hartshorne affirms a God in
which there is real potentiality. God's knowledge increases as the future becomes present. God's power has limitless opportunities for ex-
ertion. Hartshorne's God is a growing God. Now, one of the reasons
given by classical theists for denying potentiality in God is that God,
as the one who is completely unsurpassable and perfect, can lack no
perfection. But if there is potentiality in God there are perfections
which he lacks.

Hartshorne's response comes in two parts. In the first place, the
notion of a being containing all possible perfections is incoherent.
Since there are incompatible goods, not all goods (or perfections) can
be actualized.

> In every choice some good possibilities are rejected, in every
> artistic creation possible forms of beauty are renounced. (CS
> 229).

Even for the classical theist, God was faced with the decision to create
this world or some other, he could not create both. The worlds he
chose not to create were not simply valueless. Thus, in creating the
world some goods were necessarily left unactualized. Unlike Leibniz,
Hartshorne denies that the concept of a greatest possible value is any
more coherent than the possibility of a greatest possible number. A
God who contains all possible perfections is therefore impossible. (*WV*
18).

The second half of Hartshorne's response is to redefine the concept
of perfect being so as to make it intelligible. The perfect being might
be (a) unsurpassable by any being, including itself, or (b) unsurpassable
by any being other than itself but capable of surpassing itself. Classical

theism denied that God could surpass himself in perfection. Hartshorne rejects this view and defines God as the "self-surpassing surpasser of all." (DR 20). Although it is impossible for any being, other than himself, to rival God's perfection, God is capable of increase in value. The increase of value in the divine life occurs partly as a result of creaturely decisions. As noted above, each individual has some capacity for self-creation. In creating oneself one adds new definiteness to reality and hence, new value. God, in his knowledge of the new creation also acquires this new value. The beauty and moral goodness of a charitable deed, for example, contributes not only to the value of the world, but to the divine life as well. There are, of course, also negative values in the world. If God rejoices in our triumphs, he also sorrows at our pettiness, greed, and indifference. But Hartshorne believes there is always more satisfaction than dissatisfaction and thus God always has more reason for joy than sorrow. Furthermore, God retains the consciousness of past joys. Thus, "there will always be a net increment of value accruing to God at each moment." (DR 46).

A possible objection to the idea of God as the self-surpassing surpasser of all is that a being who can be surpassed by itself can also be surpassed by another. Thus, it is conceivable that some being other than God could surpass him in perfection, which is absurd. Hartshorne escapes this problem by his doctrine that God includes the world as part of himself. Hartshorne distinguishes three views of the relationship between God and the world,

> (1) God is merely the cosmos, in all aspects inseparable from the sum or system of dependent things or effects; (2) he is both the system and something independent of it; (3) he is not the system, but in all aspects independent. (DR 90).

The first view, that God and the world are identical, is pantheism. The third view is classical theism. Hartshorne adopts the second view, sometimes called panentheism. Hartshorne likens the relationship between God and the world to the relationship between a person and his or her body. A person is not simply identical with one's body. One's body undergoes constant change, but one remains the same person. Similarly, God's body, the cosmos, is constantly changing, but God remains himself. When Hartshorne says that God includes the world he means to say that the world is a part of God. Here is a clear break with the classical doctrine of divine simplicity. Further, since the world is a part of God, there is no logical possibility of a being in the world surpassing God in perfection. For whatever value a creature has, God has it too, plus something more. The divine unsurpassability (by another) is thus insured.

The analogy between the person/body relation and God/world relation has interesting ramifications for the rest of metaphysics. We have noted that Hartshorne's God is in some respects dependent on the world. But according to Hartshorne, "to be conditioned by *is* to include . . . "[20] In being conditioned by, or dependent on the world, God includes the world. But since God necessarily exists, it follows that the world necessarily exists. And indeed, this is Hartshorne's contention.[21] For Hartshorne, both God and the world necessarily exist. Dipolar theism therefore rules out the possibility affirmed by classical theism of creation *ex nihilo*.

It is important to note that, for Hartshorne, the universe is not an entity existing over against God. There is not 'God and the world', but rather, 'God and all non-divine entities'. What is normally referred to as the universe is merely the set of all nondivine entities. Although the individuals in this set have an independence of God characterized by freedom of self-creativity, the set, as a whole, has no independence. The universe is included in, or is a part of, the divine reality. "God is the self-identical individuality of the world somewhat as a man is the self-identical individuality of his ever changing system of atoms." (MVG 230). The necessity of the universe is identical with the necessity of God's existence. The necessary element in the universe is God's immanence in each nondivine event.

A consequence of the view that God is conditioned, which the Frenchman Lequier was perhaps first to see, is that, in a certain sense, we create something in God. Hartshorne notes that Lequier says,

> . . . that in making our decisions we to a certain extent make ourselves. "Thou (God) hast created me creator of myself."
> Since this partly new myself becomes an item in divine cognition, the individual creates something in God. (WV 16).

God is therefore not simply the creator, he is, to some extent created. This view is in direct opposition to classical theism which took the distinction between God and the world to correspond to the distinction between creator and created.

Classical theism involves what Hartshorne often calls a "monopolar prejudice." Hartshorne is referring to the practice of putting God on only one side (or one pole) of a pair of metaphysical contraries. Thus, according to classical theism, God is (for example) absolute, creator, infinite, and necessary while the world is relative, created, finite and contingent.[22] Hartshorne believes such a view is too simple. The truth of the matter is that God is both absolute and relative, creator and created, infinite and finite, necessary and contingent. This is what Hartshorne calls the principle of dual transcendence. It takes both sides of metaphysical contraries to describe God (CS 120). Thus, Hartshorne refers to God as being dipolar. He has a necessary pole and a contingent pole, an absolute pole and a relative pole, etc.

Some philosophers feel that Hartshorne is guilty of self-contradiction in using the principle of dual transcendence.[23] Hartshorne avoids contradiction by distinguishing various aspects in God. For example, God is not necessary and contingent in the same sense. Although God's existence is necessary (he could not not-be), the particular manner in which his existence is actualized is contingent. Thus, Hartshorne distinguishes existence from actuality. There is perhaps no other distinction as crucial as this one for understanding neoclassical theism. Hartshorne says,

> That I shall (at least probably) exist tomorrow is one thing;
> that I shall exist hearing a bluejay call at noon is another. The
> latter is the more specific or concrete statement, and it is
> not entailed by the former (unless one accepts the logical
> structure of Leibniz's theory of the monad). (LP 63).

The fact that an individual exists gives no information about the specific manner in which he or she exists. Existence is one thing, actuality quite another. Applying this distinction to the divine case we can say that, God's existence is necessary but his actuality is contingent. That God's actuality might have been different can be seen from the fact that the world might have been different. If, instead of listening to Einstein and others, Roosevelt and Truman, had, like Hitler, not given the development of the atomic bomb top priority, world history might have taken a very different course. God would then not have knowledge of the way the world is now, but the way it would have been. He would also have incorporated different values from what he actually possesses. In short, God's actuality could have been different. But whether God knows this world or one that might have been, he still exists. That God exists is necessary. That he exists with just the knowledge, feeling or value he has is contingent.

Similar remarks are applicable to the other pairs of metaphysical contraries. For example, God is absolute or independent in the sense that he exists regardless of which world is actual. But whatever world there is, God is related, and thus dependent on it (though not for his existence!). Or again, God helps create any world there is. But his actuality (not his existence) is partly created by the world. Since any actualization of value involves limitation or finitude, God is also finite. God is infinite with respect to his possibilities for actualization.[24] From these examples it is evident that no contradiction is involved in the principle of dual transcendence as long as one is careful to distinguish various aspects in God.

Classical theists failed to make the distinction between actuality and existence and thus failed to see that potentiality can be introduced into God without contradiction. Thus, Aquinas had argued that,

> The being whose substance has an admixture of potency is liable not to be by as much as it has potency; for that which can be, can not-be. But, God, being everlasting, in His substance cannot not-be. In God, therefore, there is no potency to being.[25]

As far as God's existence is concerned, Aquinas is correct. There is no possibility of God not existing. But this does not mean that there can be no potency in God. The particular state, or manner in which God exists—his actuality—is contingent and therefore contains a principle of potentiality. There is potency in God in at least two respects. In the first place, God knows the actual world. But since the world, as it is, might have been different, God's knowledge might have been different. Second, there is potency in God in the sense that God grows with the world. He has an infinite capacity to adjust to any world-state that becomes actual. Thus, the existence/actuality distinction allows Hartshorne to deny the existence of a purely immutable God without falling into the absurdity of claiming that God might have failed to exist. Potency, the capacity for being otherwise, is not found in God's existence. But God's actuality might always have been other than it is. Of course, Hartshorne denies that the divine actuality could absolutely fail to be. It is a consequence of the view that God's existence is necessary that God be somehow actualized. Otherwise, God would be a mere abstraction, not a concrete reality. But the fact (if it is a fact) that God necessarily exists does not determine the way in which that existence is actualized.

The concept of God's necessary existence has, thus far, been used rather uncritically. As we shall see in the next chapter, Hartshorne claims that God's existence must be considered logically necessary. If God exists then he exists in every conceivable state of affairs. A result of this view is what Hartshorne calls modal coincidence, or in some places, modal extensiveness. According to this doctrine, God's existence is coextensive with actuality and possibility (LP 38). God not only knows the actual world, whatever could be actual God could know as actual. Thus, if God exists, there is no conceivable state of affairs that he could not know. God is the God of the possible as well as the actual. The difference between the classical idea of *actus purus* and the neoclassical idea of modal coincidence is that the latter doctrine admits potentiality into the divine. God, as neoclassically conceived does not contain all value. But any value that could be actualized, God could contain.

Sometimes, in explaining the concept of modal coincidence, Hartshorne has spoken as if the existence of God were the explanation of logical possibility. "God himself is conceived as the ground of all possibility, presupposed by any affirmation, any possibly legitimate negation, any state of affairs, any truth." (CS 258). This has led Henry L. Ruf to claim that Hartshorne's concept of God is unintelligible.

> It is impossible for Hartshorne's God to exist because it is impossible for anything to be a necessary condition for the existence of logical possibilities as possibilities.[26]

According to Ruf, logical possibilities are not the sorts of things that need a ground. The reason is that if something is possible, it is necessarily true that it is possible.[27] A necessary truth, however, needs no ground. Thus, if Hartshorne's concept of God is the concept of a being who is the ground of logical possibility, it is impossible for such a being to exist.

Ironically, Robert Neville, has recently attacked neoclassical theism for failing to provide a sufficient explanation for metaphysical first principles. Presumably, logical truths are among the metaphysical first principles. Employing the dictum that "[w]hatever is determinately complex calls for explanation," Neville argues that, since first principles are determinately complex, they require explanation. "But with respect to the formal possibility of those universal structures, [first principles], Hartshorne's theory gives no account."[28] Whereas Ruf complains that Hartshorne attempts to explain too much by making God the ground of possibility, Neville complains that, by failing to account for metaphysical first principles, Hartshorne has not explained enough.

As far as the correct interpretation of Hartshorne's thought is concerned, Neville is much closer to the mark than Ruf. Ruf has simply read too much into Hartshorne's talk about God being the ground of possibility. Hartshorne is not attempting to explain why logical possibilities are as they are and not otherwise. They could not be otherwise and thus do not require explanation. The doctrine of modal coincidence says no more than that God's existence is coextensive with possibility as such. God exists in every possible state of affairs. This is why Hartshorne claims that the existence of God is "presupposed by any affirmation, any possible legitimate negation . . . " (CS 258). If Hartshorne's concept of God is incoherent, it is not for the reasons Ruf adduces.

Ruf's criticism is more applicable to Neville's concept of God than to Hartshorne's. Neville does seem to believe that possibility requires explanation. Indeed, this is the main thrust of his criticism of neoclassical theism. In his reply to Neville, Hartshorne makes it clear that he sees no reason to believe that metaphysical first principles stand in need of explanation.

> The most abstract definiteness or complexity I regard as necessary, for contingency just is the freedom of creativity to provide this or that instead.[29]

For Hartshorne, only contingent truths require explanation. And if the doctrine of modal coincidence is correct, then God must always be part of the explanation of any contingency. This is the only sense in which Hartshorne's God can be called the ground of possibility.

One aspect of classical theism we have yet to mention is the doctrine of the immortality of the soul. The soul, it was held, continues to exist even after bodily death. Hartshorne denies that the soul continues to exist apart from the body. Like Whitehead, Hartshorne does not rule out, a priori the possibility of survival of bodily death (RSP 143). Perhaps we survive our death, but Hartshorne does not think so. For Hartshorne this is simply not a live issue. Religiously speaking, conscious survival of bodily death is not important. Hartshorne could here invoke the example of some forms of Buddhism for which there is no continuance of an individual's consciousness after death. If Hartshorne denies the doctrine of the immortality of the soul, he does not deny immortality altogether. The kind of immortality Hartshorne espouses is called by Whitehead, objective immortality. Objective immortality is a function of God's omniscience. God knows all that is occurring and remembers all that has taken place. Unlike human memory which is fallible, indistinct, and fragmentary, God's memory is nothing less than a perfect record of the past. Although, according to Hartshorne, we must all die, we live forevermore in the memory of the divine.

Hartshorne maintains that objective immortality, not literal personal survival of bodily death, is what is religiously significant. Of all questions, religion must answer the question of the meaning of life. People want to believe that their lives have significance, that it does not all add up to zero. We wish, in some way, to contribute to something greater than ourselves. The something greater to which we contribute, in Hartshorne's metaphysics, is the divine life. In the divine memory we achieve objective immortality. And this supplies the needed significance for our lives.

> Our abiding value is indeed what we give to posterity, to the life that survives us; but is there not one who survives all deaths and for whose life all life is precious? For the believer, it is the Holy One who is our final posterity. (LP 242).

In contributing to the divine life we are contributing to something indestructible, abiding, and permanent (Hartshorne calls this view contributionism; I have called it plenarism.)[30] If we find a place in the divine memory we can be assured that whatever good we have made of our lives will not be lost. Furthermore, we are assured that God will make unsurpassably good use of our lives in a way that would have been impossible for us. Our lives have nothing less than a cosmic significance. Objective immortality is, then, taken to be an adequate response to the question of the meaning of life. Hartshorne says,

> Classical theism cannot give us hope of serving a cause infinitely greater than ourselves; for its God derived no benefit from our lives. Atheism cannot give it either; for it is limited to what we can do for posterity, which will little remember us, and our effects upon which are very incompletely predictable—quite apart from the manifest impossibility of knowing that there will always be a human posterity. The idea of objective immortality is an immense advantage of process theology over all its rivals. (WV 19).

Neoclassical theism presents modern religion with an alternative heretofore unavailable. No longer is it necessary to choose between a purely infinite God like that of the scholastics, and a purely finite

God like that of Mill. If Hartshorne is correct, then the classical insight that God is the absolute reality can be coherently combined with the deep religious intuition that God truly sympathizes with his creatures. In this chapter we have deliberately avoided an extensive discussion of the liabilities of dipolar theism. We shall have ample opportunity for this in our treatment of the global argument. For now, it is important to give neoclassical theism the courtesy of explaining itself.

IV
The Ontological Argument

Of all of the elements of Hartshorne's global argument, the ontological proof is perhaps the most important. As Hartshorne comments,

> . . . it is this argument [the ontological] that gives us the clue to the logic of any possible theistic argument.[1]

An examination of the ontological proof is therefore essential to a proper understanding of Hartshorne's *a priori* cumulative case. Goodwin's book is the best single piece on Hartshorne's ontological argument.[2] He demonstrates that the argument is tied to Hartshorne's neoclassical metaphysics, and more specifically, to the Hartshornean theory of temporal possibility. We cannot improve on Goodwin's scholarship. But we can, perhaps, throw a different light on the argument by getting clear on its relations to the other theistic proofs. In this way, it will become apparent in what sense the ontological argument is the "clue to the logic of any possible theistic argument." We will also see in what way the ontological proof relies on the others for support.

Hartshorne first discussed the ontological argument in his 1923 dissertation (*OD* 259–285). Since that time he has defended the argument perhaps more extensively than any other philosopher in history.[3] At no time, however, has the argument clearly been considered sufficient, unto itself, to establish the truth of theism. In his dissertation, the ontological proof is only the last of a multiple phase argument designed to demonstrate the existence of God. Later, in 1944 he says, "It is the coherence of arguments, not any one argument, that can decide as to God's existence."[4] A similar point is made in 1964, "It is a mistake to ask of Anselm's proof that it do everything for the defense of theism . . . "[5] Finally, in a recent reply to criticism, Hartshorne says,

> [Anselm's] goal of a single theistic argument that would make
> others unnecessary is unattainable. A whole system of basic
> ideas is required to meet all objections to his single argument.[6]

If the ontological argument does not, by itself, prove the existence of
God, it nevertheless holds a central place in Hartshorne's global argument. As noted above, Hartshorne believes that it provides the clue
to the logic of any theistic proof. To understand Hartshorne's meaning,
let us look at his version of the argument.

As is well known, Hartshorne maintains that there are two forms
of the argument found in Anselm's *Proslogion*. Norman Malcolm is
usually given credit for this discovery, but it was Hartshorne who first
came to this conclusion.[7] The Hartshorne–Malcolm reading of Anselm
has not gone unchallenged.[8] This fine point of Anselmian scholarship
need not delay our discussion. For whatever is true of Anselm, it is a
fact that something in the *Proslogian* suggested to Hartshorne that there
can be a valid ontological argument. And it is this argument which
concerns us. What is the so-called second, or stronger form of the
ontological proof? Hartshorne's first formal statement of the proof appeared in 1944.[9] Later, in 1962 (*LP* 50–51) he employed the symbolic
apparatus of modal logic to state the argument. In his book on Anselm
two forms of the argument are given (*AD* 92, 96). Another formulation
of the argument appeared in 1970 as part of the global argument (*CS*
281).[10] Most recently (1982), Hartshorne has provided a simplified
version of the argument.[11] Further refinements of the 1962 version of
the proof were made by Purtill.[12] Purtill's revision considerably sim-
plifies the proof without abandoning the essentials of Hartshorne's
version. Purtill's revision is as follows:

'q'   for '$(\exists x)Px$,' there is a perfect being, or perfec-
        tion exists.

'$\Box$'   for 'it is necessary that' or '$\sim \Diamond \sim$'.

'$\Diamond$'   for 'it is possible that' or '$\sim \Box \sim$'.

'$p \supset q$'   for 'p materially implies q' or '$\sim(p \& \sim q)$'.

'$p \rightarrow q$'   for 'p strictly implies q' or '$\Box \sim (p \& \sim q)$'.

1. $(q \rightarrow \Box q) \supset (\Diamond q \rightarrow q)$ theorem

2. $q \rightarrow \Box q$ assumption (Anselm's principle)

3. $\Diamond q \rightarrow q$ 1, 2, Modus Ponens

4. $\Diamond q$ assumption (perfection is conceiv-
                                   able, i.e., logically possible)

5.   q   3, 4, Modus Ponens

Purtill notes that the first premise is derivable from axioms of modal logic.[13] The only serious questions, then, concern the truth of the second and fourth steps. Although the second step, in a sense, requires help from other theistic arguments, it provides the key to the logic of any theistic proof. The fourth step is the weak point of the argument— the point at which the other proofs are really needed to come to the aid of the ontological proof.

The second premise says that if a perfect being exists, then a perfect being necessarily exists. Tomis Kapitan has pointed to an apparent difficulty with this premise (which he labels P1).

> (P1) states only that if *some* being is perfect then, necessarily, *some* being is perfect. Therefore (P1) does not guarantee that a being who is perfect, if there is such a being, is such that *he* is necessarily perfect, or that *he* necessarily exists, but only that there *must* be some being or other which is perfect or necessarily exists.[14]

Perhaps Kapitan has in mind the following picture. Suppose for the sake of argument that it is true that a perfect being exists. It follows, by premise (2) that there is always in existence a perfect being. But so far as premise (2) is concerned, perfect beings may pop in and out of existence at random. So long as there is some perfect being or other, it is necessarily true that a perfect being necessarily exists.

Hartshorne is aware of the kind of problem Kapitan has raised.

> If the formula '$(\exists x)Dx$' ('for some x, x is divine') the values of the variable 'x' are taken to be individuals, in the usual sense of thing or person, then 'for some x' is misleading, since only one individual could be divine. In other words, '$(\exists x)Dx$ & $(\exists y)Dy$' strictly implies '$(x = y)$'. (*AD* 50).

If, as Hartshorne says, only one individual could have been divine then Kapitan's criticism would have been answered. For if there is at most one God, then the two occurrences of 'q' in premise (2)— '$q \rightarrow \Box q$'—could not refer to more than one individual. But what reason is there for thinking there could be only one perfect being? Several reasons can be offered, two of which are discussed in chapter X. Suffice it to say that Hartshorne is not unaware of Kapitan's kind of criticism and has arguments at his disposal to solve the problem. I shall, therefore, assume throughout the remainder of this chapter that there is, at most, one perfect being.

Premise (2) is meant to be a statement of what Hartshorne calls Anselm's principle. Hartshorne says,

> The true Anselmian Principle, which so few know, that of *Prosl.* III, is, *To exist without conceivable alternative of not existing is better than to exist with such alternative*; hence Greatness is incapable of the latter. (*AD* 88).

Hartshorne probably has in mind Anselm's statement that,

> . . . it is possible to conceive of a being which cannot be conceived not to exist; and this is greater than one which can be conceived not to exist.[15]

We have, then, two possibilities with respect to the concept of any being, (1) it can be conceived not to exist, that is, as existing contingently, or (2) it cannot be conceived not to exist, that is, as existing necessarily. If necessary existence is greater than contingent existence, then, if a perfect being exists, he must exist necessarily. For if a perfect being existed contingently, it would always be possible to conceive of a more perfect being—one that exists necessarily. The exclusion of contingency from divine existence is what Hartshorne calls Anselm's discovery.

By itself, Anselm's principle does not prove that God, in fact, exists. Premise (4)—that God's existence is conceivable—is needed for a complete proof. Anselm succeeded in refuting atheism and empirical theism which hold in common the assumption that the existence and nonexistence of God are equally conceivable. But positivism, which holds that the concept of God is somehow incoherent, is not affected by Anselm's principle. Once it is conceded, however, that God is conceivable, the existence of God immediately follows. If it is true that God could not exist contingently then he must exist necessarily. And if he exists necessarily he exists—c'est tout. Another way to see this is by considering the following alternatives,

A: God exists in every conceivable state of affairs.
B: God exists in no conceivable state of affairs.
C: God exists in some conceivable states of affairs but not in others.

C is ruled out by Anselm's principle. B is the positivist position. Granting the falsity of B, A is the only remaining alternative.

Sometimes one hears the atheist retort: granted that God's existence must be considered necessary, it does not follow that God exists. All that has been shown is that, *if* God exists, then necessarily he exists. Hartshorne and Malcolm believe this statement harbors a contradiction. Hartshorne comments:

> "If God exists, he exists noncontingently" I regard as self-contradictory; for the "if" can only mean that something which could be lacking is required for the existence, while "noncontingently" means that nothing required for the existence could possibly fail, or have failed to obtain. "If" refers to a condition, but we are speaking of unconditioned existence. Thus "if" and "necessary" do not properly combine in the manner proposed.[16]

"If" implies the possibility of God's nonexistence, whereas "necessary" implies the impossibility of God's nonexistence. Given the truth of Anselm's principle, the only meaning "if" can have in the statement "If God exists he necessarily exists" is to refer to our own ignorance. Properly stated, the sentence reads: If God exists, and we're not sure if he does, then he necessarily exists. Our uncertainty concerns the question of whether the concept of God makes sense: Is the concept of God coherent?

Needless to say, not everyone agrees that Hartshorne's reasoning is cogent. Most would agree that God, if he exists, has an unusual mode of existing, different from ordinary existence. But they would not call this extraordinary existence necessary in the sense of logically necessary. John Hick has long criticized Hartshorne for what Hick claims is a confusion between two kinds of necessity, ontological (or factual necessity) and logical necessity.[17] The ontological argument is invalid, according to Hick, since it equivocates between these two concepts of necessity. According to Hick,

> . . . to say that God has (logically) necessary being, or that his existence is logically necessary, would be to say that the meaning of "God" is such that the proposition "God exists" is a logical, analytic or a priori truth; or again that the proposition "God does not exist" is a self-contradiction, a statement of such a kind that it is logically impossible for it to be true.[18]

The heart of the idea of ontological necessity is what has come to be called existence *a se*, or aseity. Existence *a se* refers to,

> . . . the existence of something that simply and unqualifiedly
> *is*, without beginning or end and without dependence for
> its existence or for its characteristics upon anything other than
> itself.[19]

Hick believes that it is the idea of ontological necessity, not logical
necessity, which Anselm was indicating when he said that God cannot
be conceived not to exist. Furthermore—and here is the crux of Hick's
critique—if God's existence is only ontologically necessary, then God's
nonexistence is possible. But if God's nonexistence is possible then
the ontological argument must fail, since God's existence, like all other
existence, would be conceptually contingent. In terms of the alternatives listed on page 48, Hick would choose C: God exists in some
conceivable states of affairs but not in others.

Similar criticisms of the second form of Anselm's argument have
been raised by Lycan and Plantinga.[20] Plantinga says,

> If God cannot (logically) come into or go out of existence, it
> is a necessary truth that if He ever exists, He always exists.
> But it does not follow that if He exists, the proposition "God
> exists" is logically necessary.[21]

Plantinga's point is that even if God's existence is ontologically necessary, it does not follow, without further argument, that his existence
is logically necessary. Of course, further argument has been given as
we shall see. But most philosophers who speak in terms of God's ontologically necessary being do so in order to emphasize their belief that
God's existence is not logically necessary. In other words, they maintain that God's existence, if he exists, is logically contingent.

Hartshorne is aware of Hick's criticism, but insists that there is no
firm basis for a distinction between ontological and logical modalities.

> Anselm's conviction was, and mine is, that only the concep-
> tually necessary can reasonably be viewed as uncaused, and
> only the conceivably caused can reasonably be viewed as con-
> ceptually contingent.[22]

Hartshorne supports this view by his theory of temporal possibility,
according to which,

> Modal distinctions are ultimately coincident with temporal

ones. The actual is the past, the possible is the future.
(CS 60).

Hartshorne is, therefore, concerned not to drive a wedge between the modal operators "$\square$" and "$\lozenge$" and the temporal structure of existence. On this view, to say something is logically possible is to say it might have occurred in the past (since all past moments were once future) or that it might occur in the future. Hartshorne says, "nothing has even a logically possible alternative unless it was once future."[23] If Hartshorne is correct then it follows from God's aseity that God exists of logical necessity. To exist *a se* means to have no beginning and no end. Thus, if God exists, there was never a future (in the past) and there never will be a future when God might fail to exist. If no future contains the possibility of God's nonexistence, then, on Hartshorne's view, God's existence is logically necessary.

The theory of temporal possibility supplies the needed premise to infer logical necessity from ontological necessity. To deny the theory, says Hartshorne, is to make God an arbitrary exception to otherwise generally applicable rules concerning contingent existence. If the existence of God is held to be contingent then,

> . . . unlike all noncontroversially contingent propositions,
> ["God exists"] does not affirm an existence having a conceiv-
> able cause, or a conceivable beginning in time, does not
> exclude any positive form of existence or particular finite
> quantity or degree between zero and infinity, or assert any par-
> ticular kinds or numbers of parts, etc. Thus all the criteria
> that render intelligible a distinction between possible and real
> existence are lacking in this case.[24]

The same point is made in another place where Hartshorne lists ten marks of contingency and finds that none of them apply to God as the empiricists conceive him (*LP* 73–84). The point is that for any characteristic of ordinary contingent propositions, the proposition that God exists lacks these characteristics. Thus, the proposition that God exists cannot reasonably be taken as contingent.

Rather than run through all of the marks of contingent propositions, let us focus upon one characteristic of contingency, namely, that causal conditioning is always associated with contingency (understanding 'cause' as explained in chapter III). Hartshorne comments,

> We do not seek causal explanations of noncontingent truths,
> as in mathematics, but we do seek them for contingent

2141666

truths. The empiricists tell us in effect to forget all this when
considering God. They accuse Anselm of violating rules;
but they violate the elementary rule that logically contingent
matters are intelligible in genetic and causal terms, or not
at all.[25]

If it were possible for Hartshorne's opponents to produce one example (besides "God exists") of a logically contingent existential statement, inexplicable in causal terms, there might be some precedent
for denying the logical necessity of God's existence. But the only
examples that are offered are highly suspect. Gaunilo spoke of a lost
island, Paul Henle of "Necs," William Rowe of an eternal star, and
William Lycan of "agnews" or eternal gavels.[26] The idea behind all
of these examples is to think of something ordinarily considered contingent and apply to it the property of being eternal—or in our language, existing *a se*.

If the examples are successful, they demonstrate that an eternal
being could exist contingently. Rowe says,

> Surely it is possible for an everlasting star to exist. The stars
> that exist are presumably not everlasting—for each star, let
> us suppose, there was a time before which it did not exist
> and there will be a time at which it ceases to exist. But this
> seems to be an empirical fact and not a matter of conceptual or
> logical necessity.[27]

We must differ with Rowe; it is no mere empirical fact that there are
no everlasting stars. For an everlasting star would not be a star as we
understand the term. An everlasting star would not, for example,
consume the gases of which it is made. And if it consumed no gases
it could give off no light. In short, an everlasting star is not a star at
all. Similar comments could be made with regard to the other examples. If Gaunilo's lost island does not depend for its continued
existence on the sea level, the nonoccurence of earthquakes, erosion,
etc., then it is not really an island. Implied in the very idea of an
island or a star is the concept of contingency, and of noneternal
existence. Whatever we describe as being logically contingent—except the empiricist's God—is explicable in causal terms. We, therefore, agree with Hartshorne, that to allow that God exists *a se* is to
imply that his existence is logically necessary. The burden of proof
rests with Hick and company to explain how their God is not an
exception to the rules of contingency. Of course, our argument pre-

supposes that, as Whitehead says, "God is not to be treated as an exception to all metaphysical principles . . . "[28] But what empiricist would self-consciously deny this?[29]

One of the chief arguments for classifying "God exists" as contingent hails from British empiricism. According to Hume, "Whatever we conceive as existent, we can also conceive as nonexistent."[30] It follows that no existential proposition can be logically necessary. Thus, if God exists, the proposition expressing the fact must be logically contingent.

Hartshorne offers as counter-examples to Hume's claim that all propositions expressing existence are contingent the following: "Something exists." (CS 161), "There is a universe." (cf. *PSG* 435), and "Some particular things actually exist." (*IO* 143). In the following chapter we consider Hartshorne's arguments for the necessity of there being a universe. Some philosophers, however, do not deny that these statements are necessary but only that they have existential import. For example, Kai Nielsen maintains that Hartshorne's proposition,

(1)   There is a universe

is either nonsense or a tautology.[31] Nielsen claims that if 'universe' is synonymous with 'all the things there are' then (1) becomes "There is all the things there are" or more grammatically,

(2)   There are all the things there are.

If 'There are' means 'exists' then (2) is a veiled form of the tautology "All the things that exist exist." On the other hand, says Nielsen, "We have nonsense if 'There are' functions as it does when we exclaim 'There are all the Beatles together'."[32]

Nielsen's argument turns on a rather incautious construal of (1). It is significant that Nielsen's translation omits the article 'a'. For the universe that exists is not the only universe that could exist—it is *a* universe. This means that 'a universe' is not synonymous with 'all the things there are' (although it is synonymous with 'the universe'). Nielsen's translation of (1) is therefore inadequate. For this reason he has failed to prove that "there is a universe" lacks existential import. Since, as Nielsen admits, "There is a universe" appears to be an existential proposition, it stands as a challenge to the empiricist's denial that there can be necessary existential statements.

The discussion thus far has yielded the conclusion that contingency must be excluded from God's existence. This is Anselm's principle.

What has not been shown is that the concept of God does not conceal an absurdity. God's existence might be logically impossible. Thus, from Anselm's principle alone we can deduce only that God's existence is either logically necessary or logically impossible. The importance of Anselm's principle, however, is that it provides the key to the logic of theism. Theism can no longer be considered simply as a question of fact, questions of meaning are at stake. God's existence is a conceptual problem.

> Self-understanding is the issue: someone is confused, either
> the theist, or the nontheist. Which is it? This is the real ques-
> tion. (NT 88).

For this reason, Hartshorne maintains that empirical arguments for (or against) the existence of God are impossible. Before this claim can be evaluated we must understand what Hartshorne means by an "empirical argument for theism."

Hartshorne adopts Popper's position that falsifiability by some conceivable experience is a minimal requirement of the empirical. What, then, is an empirical argument? At one point Hartshorne identifies an empirical argument as any argument whose premises are empirical (CS 278). Elsewhere, empirical arguments are identified as having an empirically falsifiable conclusion. Thus, in connection with the so-called empirical arguments for God's existence Hartshorne asks,

> . . . what advocate of 'empirical arguments' for theism (Ten-
> nant? Brightman?) has told us how experience might conceiv-
> ably show that God does not exist? (NT 67).

Does Hartshorne mean to define an empirical argument by reference to its premises or to its conclusion? The answer to this question seems important. For if an empirical argument is any argument with empirical premises then it seems there could be an empirical argument for God's existence. For example, an argument from authority to God's existence would have an empirical premise to the effect that so-and-so is a reliable authority.[33] On the other hand, if an empirical argument is identified by an experientially falsifiable conclusion, then Hartshorne is correct in asserting the impossibility of an empirical argument for God's existence. According to Anselm's principle, if God exists, then he exists without conceivable alternative. And this just means that nothing could falsify the proposition "God exists."

I am inclined to believe Hartshorne means to identify empirical arguments by their conclusions. When he claims that none of the theistic proofs have empirical premises he has in mind the traditional proofs such as the cosmological and design arguments. According to Hartshorne, it is not simply a fact that contingent beings exist or that there is order; these are necessary truths. A totally chaotic world or a world in which nothing exists are not conceivable. Thus, the premises of these arguments are not genuinely empirical. Furthermore, arguments from authority are useful only when the authorities themselves do not disagree or when the person advocating the argument is not one of the authorities. But as with most philosophic disputes, theism has no agreed upon solution. And the people who offer arguments for God's existence (and those to whom they are directed) are usually authorities on the subject anyway. Thus, there is little hope for arguments from authority in this issue. Anselm's principle casts doubt on the fruitfulness of attempting to infer God's existence from empirical premises.

One final criticism of the ontological argument must be considered. B. G. Nowlin and R. L. Purtill have criticized the argument for being "sound, but superfluous."[34] Neither author disagrees with the concept of God as logically necessary being. But both believe that,

> . . . one could have sufficient reason for thinking the ontological argument sound only by employing some other proof which would render the ontological argument superfluous.[35]

The weak premise in the ontological argument is the premise which says that God is conceivable. But how is this to be demonstrated? Purtill notes that one way to prove the conceivability of God is to prove that God exists. But this renders the ontological argument superfluous, since we would have proved the existence of God without it. The other way to prove the conceivability of God is to show that some conceivable state of affairs contains the divine—heaven perhaps. The task of the atheist would be to show that some conceivable state of affairs lacks the divine. The problem with this strategy is that conceivability is such a tricky matter. We have already seen, in this chapter, how easy it is to combine contradictory ideas without realizing there is a contradiction, e.g., eternal stars and lost islands. Purtill and Nowlin believe the most promising strategy for theists is to prove the conceivability of God by proving that God exists. Thus, even if the ontological argument is sound, it is superfluous.

Even if, in a certain sense, the ontological argument is superfluous, in another sense it represents a tremendous gain in philosophic understanding. Hartshorne admits that any

> proof which establishes the conceivability of God can as well or better be so formulated that it directly establishes his existence.[36]

To this extent the ontological argument is superfluous. But there are at least three senses in which it is not superfluous

One often hears atheists claim that the burden of proof is on the theist since the theist is the one who is introducing a novel entity to explain things.[37] Such a demand is unjustified in light of the ontological argument. God cannot be, in Tillich's words, one being among others; he is rather, the very condition of there being anything or any truth at all. The problem of God's existence is not empirical, it is conceptual. As far as God's existence is concerned, all the facts are in, and all the relevant explanations have been given. What remains to be seen is whether the theist or the nontheist is conceptually confused. There is no neutral ground on which the atheist can hide. For in the very assertion that God does not exist, concepts are employed. Either these concepts require or they exclude the existence of God. In either case the atheist is as much obliged as the theist to defend his or her position—the theist to argue for, the atheist to argue against the conceptual necessity for God.

Another important function of the ontological argument is that it demonstrates that the traditional problem of evil is a confusion. Implicit in the atheistic argument from evil is the assumption that God is equally conceivable as existent or nonexistent. We are told that, if God existed, he would prevent a great deal of the suffering in the world. But what is this but an admission that the atheist can conceive of a world in which God exists? Anselm's principle should change such atheists into theists! The ontological argument at least shows that the only respectable argument from evil is a priori, that is, that the mere conceivability of suffering contradicts the existence of God.

Finally, the ontological argument shows that any theistic argument which begins from a premise to the effect that the world requires God in some way, must also admit that any conceivable world or coherently conceivable absence of a world would require God if the divine existence is necessary. If the existence of certain contingent beings requires that God exists, then any conceivable world with contingent beings requires God. Similarly, if the existence of order is a mark of the creator's handywork, then any ordered world or any to a coherently conceivable degree disordered world would bear God's imprint. The arguments that Nowlin or Purtill would offer for God's conceivability (and thus existence), at least depend upon the ontological argument for this point of clarification. To admit the validity of the ontological argument, therefore, represents a net gain in philosophical theology.

The importance of the Nowlin-Purtill objection is that it raises, once again, the spectre of positivism. The weakest premise of the ontological argument is premise (4)—that God is conceivable. Hartshorne says of this premise,

> All my difficulty in believing in theism, all of it, turns on the not easily disproved suspicion that every available formulation of the idea of God involves some more or less well hidden absurdity.[38]

The justification of God's conceivability rests with considerations properly outside the ontological argument—in short, with the other theistic proofs. It is to these we now turn.

V
The Cosmological Argument

The cosmological argument appears several places in Hartshorne's work. The "Argument from the Category of Being," of his 1923 dissertation, is arguably the first presentation of the proof (*OD* 99–116). In *Man's Vision of God* (1941), an entire chapter is devoted to the argument (*MVG* 251–298). In 1953, the proof is included as one of the six ways to demonstrate God's existence (*PSG* 24–25). By the time of *Creative Synthesis* (1970), the six arguments become elements of the one global argument, wherein the cosmological proof is a part (*CS* 275–297). Each discussion of the cosmological argument differs in important respects from the others; and it is not clear that the various forms in which Hartshorne offers the proof are reducible to one another. For example, the 1923 version argues from the concept of Being to the reality of an all-inclusive, or monistic One. The object of the argument in *Man's Vision of God* is to show that the most adequate conception of the subject of all change is the conception of deity neoclassically conceived. The argument of *Creative Synthesis* makes no mention of God as the subject of change. Finally, as noted in chapter II, the 1923 version of the argument is found nowhere else in Hartshorne's writings. The title of this chapter is therefore misleading; there is more than one Hartshornean cosmological argument. Despite these dissimilarities, however, there is a continuity running through the proofs. Each of the earlier versions may be viewed as contributing something to the argument of *Creative Synthesis*. Hartshorne's mature position can be seen as an attempt to incorporate, in one argument, the insights embodied in his earlier discussions. This chapter, accordingly, treats the earlier versions of the proof only as they contribute to the argument of *Creative Synthesis*. Untangling the differences between Hartshorne's cosmological arguments is a task left to others.

Following the procedure of exhausting all possible alternatives to theism, Hartshorne states the argument as follows:

A1 Nothing exists.

A2 What exists either (a) has no modal character or (b) is wholly contingent.

A3 What exists is wholly necessary.

A4 What exists is partly contingent and partly necessary, but nothing is divine.

T   What exists is partly contingent and partly necessary and something is divine. (CS 281).

Several clarifications are needed for a proper understanding of the argument.

When Hartshorne uses the words "necessary" and "contingent" he means them to be taken in a strictly logical sense. As noted in the previous chapter, Hartshorne holds to a theory of modality according to which logical and ontological modalities are not ultimately separable. To exist contingently is to exist as one among a variety of logical possibilities. To be logically possible is to be 'really' (or ontologically) possible either at some past moment or at some future time. The logically necessary is the common element in all contingencies (CS 246). This is important since it explains why Hartshorne believes his statement of the cosmological argument exhausts the possible alternatives to theism. Many theists would accept A2(b), with the proviso that there is a God whose existence is ontologically, though not logically, necessary. The conclusion of the last chapter, if true, shows that this position is mistaken. God exists of logical necessity or his existence is impossible. The position that God's existence is logically contingent is, according to Hartshorne, inconsistent with the implications of the concept of deity. A2(b) is, therefore, not an option open to theists.

It is arguable that A3 divides into two different positions, one which says that the necessary is not divine, the other that it is divine. The latter position is a form of pantheism, best exemplified by Spinoza's necessitarianism. Parmenidean monism is perhaps the nearest any philosophical system has come to denying contingency to the real while failing to identify the One with God. But the cases of Parmenides and Spinoza are unclear and could be argued either way with some plausibility. As Hartshorne says, "Spinoza has been called 'God-intoxicated' and also 'atheist'. There is a fairly strong case for both descriptions" (NT 2). Could the same apply to Parmenides? There is good reason to believe that the debate of whether an unrestricted monism is theistic or atheistic is purely verbal. One may adopt a 'worshipful' attitude towards the One and call the object of devotion "God," but I see no rational compulsion to do so.

Hartshorne's cosmological argument differs from traditional formulations not only in being nonempirical, but also in not being an argument to a prime mover, or first cause. Commentators have generally agreed that most famous versions of the argument (for example, those of Aquinas, Descartes and Clarke) are empirical.[1] Like all of Hartshorne's theistic arguments, the cosmological proof is offered as an *a priori* demonstration. Moreover, Hartshorne's version makes no mention of a first cause; it is, rather, an argument "from the modal structure of the concept of existence . . . " (CS 294).[2] The reason for classifying Hartshorne's argument as cosmological is that, in a sense (to be explained), it moves from the concept of contingently existing beings to the concept of a necessary being. With these clarifications in mind, let us examine the argument step by step.

No one doubts that the proposition "Nothing exists" is false. The more interesting question is whether "Nothing exists" describes a conceivable state of affairs. The question is not whether the proposition is false, but whether it is necessarily false. Hartshorne maintains that nonbeing, or total nothingness, is not genuinely conceivable. For Hartshorne, it is necessarily true that something or other exists. This is not to say that what exists, exists of necessity. As noted in the last chapter, any number of a variety of universes might exist. Houstin Craighead has rendered a valuable contribution to the debate by listing six arguments found in Hartshorne's writings for the necessity of something existing (I find at least eight).[3] Considerations of space and the scope of the present work do not permit a treatment of each argument. We will focus on the arguments on which Hartshorne most often relies.

The most important reason for denying the conceivability of nonbeing is that it is completely unknowable. Like Peirce, Hartshorne equates knowability with being (see chapter VI). To be capable of existing is to be knowable and to be knowable is to possibly exist. If this is correct then nonbeing is not a genuine possibility. No conceivable knower, not even an omniscient one, could know nonbeing.

This argument rests on the assumption that knowability and being are coextensive. Craighead accuses Hartshorne of arbitrarily defining being in terms of knowability. "Hartshorne has won the game by definition. He *defines* the real in terms of the knowable."[4] Craighead's contention is unfounded. Hartshorne gives reasons for the assumption in question, the most important of which Craighead never considers. Hartshorne argues that any statement which is, in principle verifiable but not falsifiable is necessarily true. Also, any statement which is falsifiable but not verifiable is necessarily false. As noted above, not even an omniscient being could verify "Nothing exists"; and it is falsified by every being that has ever existed or will exist. Thus, according to the Hartshornean criteria of necessary truth, "Nothing exists" is necessarily false.

Several reasons for thinking the criteria capture what we want to say about necessary truth and falsity can be adduced. First, the clearest examples we have of necessary falsehoods are also falsifiable but not verifiable. The existence of round-squares, unborn mortals, or polygamous bachelors are logically impossible. Their existence is not only unverifiable but also falsifiable. The mere concept of a round-square is enough to falsify its existence. Second, there are no clear counterexamples to Hartshorne's criteria. John Hick maintains that the proposition that we survive death is verifiable if true but not falsifiable if false since no one would be around to falsify it.[5] Hick would be correct if he only said that an afterlife is not falsifiable by ordinary means. But ordinary methods of falsification do not exhaust the possibilities. God might, for example, reveal to humans that there is no afterlife. Furthermore, God's own experience is capable of falsifying the existence of an afterlife. Thus, it is not true that survival of death is unfalsifiable.

A more plausible counterexample to Hartshorne's criteria is given by Hick,

> Consider, for example, the proposition that "there are three successive sevens in the decimal determination of π." So far as the value of π has been worked out, it does not contain a series of three sevens, but it will always be true that such a series may occur at a point not yet reached in anyone's calculations. Accordingly, the proposition may one day be verified if it is true, but can never be falsified if it is false.[6]

Once again it is important to distinguish between human (or nondivine) and divine capacity to falsify a proposition. In order to know the value of π, humans are obliged to actually do the requisite division. Temporal limitations preclude ever knowing the complete value of a transcendental number. But God is an eternal being—temporally unlimited. This might mean that the divine life extends infinitely into the past and indefinitely into the future. In that case God would not face the nondivine limitations in knowing the value of π. One may

also question the legitimacy of conceiving God's knowledge of mathematical, logical, and geometric truths as in any way similar to nondivine knowledge of these truths. Humans are obliged to learn that 7
+ 5 = 12, but this may be 'innate' knowledge for God. Whether
because of his infinite past life or because of an 'innate' knowledge of
abstract truths, it seems that God's experience could falsify, if false,
the proposition that three successive sevens occur in the decimal determination of π. This means that we have yet to discover a counter-
example to Hartshorne's criteria for necessary truth and falsity. Since,
according to these criteria, "Nothing exists" is necessarily false, there
is good reason to believe nonbeing is not genuinely conceivable.

Although he denied the coherence of the idea of nonbeing, Bergson
suggested a way, that has appealed to many, of conceiving complete
nothingness.

> There is, in fact, not a single object of our experience that we
> cannot suppose annihilated. Extend this annihilation of a
> first object to a second, then a third, and so on as long as you
> please: the nought (nonbeing) is the limit toward which the
> operation tends. And the nought so defined is the annihilation
> of everything.[7]

According to this view, if we take the denial of each statement asserting the existence of some object in the world and combine these
statements in a lengthy conjunction we have the meaning of "Nothing
exists."

This argument for the coherence of the concept of nonbeing com-
mits the fallacy of composition. It does not follow from our ability to
deny the existence of any particular thing within the universe that we
can deny the existence of the universe as a whole. Moreover, as Hartshorne argues, what makes a negative statement true is something
positive.

> "No food in the refrigerator" does not mean, and is not known
> to be true by observing, *nothing* in the refrigerator. We know
> it by observing the back wall of the interior or the shelves in
> such a way that would not be possible were there solid or
> liquid foods on the shelves. Mere nothing plays no such role
> as that of making negative statements true. (*OT* 81).

Defenders of the idea of nonbeing could perhaps make a persuasive
argument that statements denying the existence of fictional characters

carry no positive implications.[8] It is not clear what difference the nonexistence of leprechauns makes in the actual world. But we have a fairly good idea that (and how) the nonexistence of actually existing things makes a difference. Suppose the Pope were, tomorrow, to disappear from the face of the earth leaving no clue as to his whereabouts. On a mundane level this would mean that his bed would not be slept in, certain documents would go unsigned, appointments would go unattended, etc. The social and political scene would also change. Suspicion would arise between heads of state that a conspiracy was afoot, the church machinery would be put into action to find a new Pope, and thousands would mourn the loss of their religious leader. Although the details of his absence are unpredictable, it is evident that the Pope's disappearance would not be a purely negative fact. The same truth holds, in principle, for any other actually existing thing. The nonexistence of pebbles, drops of water and the like would be less spectacular than the nonexistence of the Pope but no less real in their effects on the world. Thus, statements denying the existence of things within the world have implicit positive implications. Unless this fact can be remedied, it is a mistake to suppose that the possibility of denying the existence of each thing within the world makes possible a denial of Being as such.

Hartshorne suggests one other argument against the concept of nonbeing worth mentioning (if only because Craighead overlooks it). He asks, "If nothing were to exist, what would make this true? Bare nothing?" (CS 159). The principle implied by this question is that the truth of a proposition is determined by a state of affairs. There being a flower in the garden makes the statement "There is a flower in the garden" true. If the flower wilts or in some other way is destroyed, the statement becomes false. In either case, truth and falsity are founded upon what is the case. But if this principle is sound then there is no way "Nothing exists" could be true. For, by hypothesis, there would be no world, no state of affairs, to make it true. To reply by calling nonbeing a state of affairs is to confuse the issues. Nonbeing is not a state of affairs. It is, rather, a denial that there are states of affairs. If nonbeing is a state of affairs, then what is the difference between "The state of affairs, nonbeing, exists" and "There are no states of affairs"? This is a distinction without a difference. We conclude, therefore, that no state of affairs could make "Nothing exists" a true statement. But a statement which could not conceivable be true is necessarily false.

We have seen several reasons for thinking that nonbeing is a pseudo-concept. But thus far, the discussion has failed to reveal an important ambiguity in the proposition "Nothing exists." The statement may mean (a) nothing nondivine exists or (b) nothing nondivine or divine exists. The arguments against the coherence of the concept of nonbeing, if sound, show that (b) is not a genuine possibility. Something, whether divine or nondivine, must exist. But it does not follow that (a) is necessarily false. It may be that "Something exists" is necessarily true but that the universe could fail to exist. Many theists hold that God could have chosen not to create a world. In that case, God would have existed but nondivine things would not. Since Hartshorne's theism requires that some nondivine things have always existed, the traditional view must be refuted. The problem can be approached from two angles, from the standpoint of the world and from the standpoint of the divine. The first is to ask whether *all* nondivine things could fail to exist. This question will involve us in the problem of the eternity of the world. The second angle from which to examine the problem is to ask whether any sense can be made of the concept of God existing without some world or other. I will argue that, (1) the debate between what I call finitism and infinitism concerning the eternity of the world is a stalemate, but (2) the concept of God existing without some world or other is not genuinely meaningful.

An important objection to the idea that the world has always existed is that the concept of an actually infinite series of events in time is contradictory or paradoxical. Wishing to preserve the doctrine of creation *ex nihilo*, arguments concerning the impossibility of an actual infinite have been favorites among Jewish, Christian and Islamic philosophers. The Christian theologian, John Philoponus, was probably the first to use the argument.[9] He was followed by an impressive list of philosophers, not the least of whom was St. Bonaventure.[10] Recently, the argument has been revised in light of modern transfinite mathematics by William Lane Craig.[11]

There are several arguments against the idea of an actually infinite series of events in time. Kant's first antinomy is a good example.

> If we assume that the world has no beginning in time, then up to every given moment an eternity has elapsed, and there has passed away in the world an infinite series of successive states of things. Now the infinity of a series consists in the fact that it can never be completed through successive synthesis. It thus follows that it is impossible for an infinite world-series to

have passed away, and that a beginning of the world is therefore a necessary condition of the world's existence.[12]

Hartshorne has long recognized the problems that arguments like this
pose for his philosophy and seems never to have answered the arguments to his complete satisfaction," . . . I confess myself puzzled in
the matter." (CS 235).[13] Hartshorne is not alone. As Craig points
out, "Contemporary philosophers have proved impotent to refute this
reasoning."[14]

It would be a mistake, to conclude from the inability of philosophers
to answer the problems posed by the idea of an actual infinite, that
one should not believe that the past is actually infinite. As noted in
Chapter I, no metaphysical worldview is without its problems. As long
as the problems in other positions are seen as greater than the problems
in one's own position, there is justification for not capitulating to the
opponent's arguments. This is Hartshorne's principle of least paradox.
"One must decide which paradoxes are the really fatal ones, in com-
parison with those of contending positions." (CS 88). This is an important principle for evaluating the debate about the actual infinite
since it can be demonstrated that there are at least as many (if not
more) problems with the idea of a beginning of time as with the idea
of a temporal infinite.

Hartshorne mentions two problems with the idea of a first moment
of time in Man's Vision of God. First, he argues:

> Even a beginning is a change, and all change requires some-
> thing changing that does not come to exist through that
> same change. The beginning of the world would have to hap-
> pen to something other than the world, something which
> as the subject of happening would be in a time that did not
> begin with the world. (MVG 233).

The other problem with the idea of a first temporal moment which
Hartshorne mentions is that a first moment would never appear to be
the first moment. An analogy with present day defenders of "Creation
Science" illustrates the point. Because they believe the universe is so
young, defenders of "Creation Science" are obliged to hold that God
created the light from distant stars half way to earth to make it appear
as though the light originated from the star. A similar paradox infects
the view that there was a first moment of time. Since any event will
appear to have come from some previous event, the so-called first
event will never look like the first event. As Russell says, for all we

know, God could have created the world five minutes ago.[15] The universe must always appear older than it actually is. "A first moment of time would be an ontological lie through and through, a joke of existence upon itself." (MVG 234).

A problem with the idea that the universe's past is temporally finite which Hartshorne does not mention, is that, whatever age the universe is, it could not be conceived to be older. St. Bonaventure recognized this as a consequence of his view. According to Bonaventure, God was not free to make this world any older than it actually is.[16] To claim that the universe could have begun, say, two seconds earlier is to imply a measure of time outside the universe. But, according to Bonaventure, the first moment of creation marks the beginning of time. Hence, there could be no time independent of the world. Nothing seems easier, however, than to imagine scientists discovering that the universe has existed for a longer time than previously believed. Of course, Bonaventure does say that it is *this* world that could not have been older. Perhaps God could have created another world, older than this one. The problem with this line of argument is that it presupposes a measure of time, independent of both worlds, in terms of which one world is said to be older than the other. But if, as Bonaventure holds, time begins with the creation of the world, then there is no independent standard of temporal duration.

Since the finitist's postion is no less paradoxical than the infinitist's position, it is reasonable to declare the debate surrounding the possibility of an actual infinite a stalemate. There is, however, one important consideration which favors the infinitist's position. It is noteworthy that in Craig's discussion of this issue (the most careful in recent literature), there is no attempt to prove that there is a contradiction in the idea of an actual infinite. Craig's position is clear.

> What I shall argue is that while the actual infinite may be a fruitful and consistent concept in the mathematical realm, it cannot be translated from the mathematical world into the real world, for this would involve counter-intuitive absurdities.[17]

In order to argue that the concept of an actual infinite is contradictory, it would be necessary to become embroiled in the debate between mathematicians concerning the legitimacy of transfinite numbers. Craig is one of the few philosophers to have understood this point. Since, as Craig notes, the majority opinion in matematical circles clearly favors the consistency of transfinite numbers, Craig steers a safe course in arguing only for the paradoxical or counterintuitive consequences of applying the concept of the actual infinite to the real world. The weight of authority in mathematics is presently against the idea that the concept of the actual infinite is contradictory. This fact can only favor the infinitist's position in the philosophical dispute concerning the eternity of the world. Both the finitist and the infinitist positions involve, in Craig's words, counterintuitive absurdities. Given the present state of mathematical knowledge, however, only the infinitist can, with any assurance, claim that there is no contradiction in his or her position.

I have argued that the debate concerning the eternity of the world is a stalemate. Both positions result in paradoxes. Insofar, then, Hartshorne's position is in no better standing than any of the alternatives (except for the proviso that it is reasonable to believe that infinitism is free of inconsistency). Let us turn, therefore, to the problem of conceiving of God as existing without a world. Hartshorne offers two arguments that God requires some world or other, one which I find inconclusive, the other which I find convincing.

The argument to which Hartshorne most often refers is from the nature of creativity. Not even God, according to Hartshorne, has the option not to create.

> Suppose [God] had refrained from creating: the world would then not have existed; however, something else would also have existed, the decision itself. There would instead have been the decision not to create, or to create some world other than ours. This shows us that a free agent must create something *in himself*, even if he decides not to create anything else; for the decision, if free, is itself a creation (CS 9).

Hartshorne speaks as if God could have chosen not to create the world. But it is clear that he does not think this is genuinely possible. A further analysis of the concept of creativity shows that creation requires antecedently given data.

> We know creativity only as a responding to prior stimuli, and if we refuse to allow an analogy between such ordinary creative action and the divine 'creating' of the cosmos, we are using a word whose meaning we cannot provide (CS 12).

Hartshorne is raising a familiar objection to the doctrine of creation *ex nihilo.* If the idea of creation is to have any recognizable meaning, then the divine form of creativity must bear some analogy to ordinary examples of creativity. But the doctrine of creation *ex nihilo* posits an absolute difference between divine and nondivine creation. If God's creativity requires antecedently given data and if God does not have the choice not to create, then the concept of God existing without a world is not genuinely conceivable.

I agree with Hartshorne that God must create, if only a new state of himself. But I am unconvinced by the argument that there is no basis for an analogy between creation *ex nihilo* and ordinary creativity. It is not inconceivable that I should discover, within myself, the power to create certain objects merely by 'willing' their existence. Whenever I 'will' that there should be a penny in my desk drawer I discover that a penny appears there.[18] Humans do not, as a matter of fact, possess this ability. But there does not appear to be any inconsistency in imagining the possibility. It is on some such analogy that creation *ex nihilo* would have to be understood.

The argument from the nature of creativity is unsuccessful. But Hartshorne suggests another argument which holds more promise for proving that God could not exist without some world or other.

> And is not the notion of a knower knowing only himself absurd? Could even God observe a mere privation? I hold that we have no right to suppose this, since we have no idea what he would be observing as the objective situation.[19]

While there can be an analogy between creation from nothing and other conceivable kinds of creativity, there is no corresponding analogy between ordinary cases of self-knowledge and the putative divine knowledge of self. Humans are incurably social creatures whose self-knowledge is set against the backdrop of something that is not the self. A child has no clear knowledge of herself until she begins to distinguish her own individuality from the environment in which she is situated. Without such an environment of something that is "not-self," it is not clear how she could ever have self-knowledge. Unlike the child's knowledge of self, God's self-knowledge has no genesis. Since there is never a time when God does not know himself, he *does not learn* to distinguish himself from the world. The important point, however, is that there seems to be a connection between self-knowledge and knowledge of the not-self. Experience furnishes no examples to the contrary.

The classical theist's reply to this argument is that God's knowledge of the not-self is different from ordinary examples of this kind of knowledge in that God's knowledge creates its objects. If knowledge of an effect is known in the cause, then, in knowing himself, God knows things other than himself. We have already discussed the reasons why Hartshorne believes this view of God's knowledge is mistaken (cf. Chapter III). Unless absolute determinism is true, knowledge of causes does not entail knowledge of the precise details of the effects. However, even allowing the truth of determinism, the traditional view of God's knowledge of the world does not answer the question with which we are concerned. The claim is that self-knowledge requires knowledge of the not-self. The question, then, is how God could have knowledge of himself if there were no world. It is no reply to this question to say that because God creates the world he knows the world. The assumption of the question is that God has not yet created the world. Prior to creating the world, God could have no knowledge of a not-self since, by hypothesis, there is no not-self. Thus, even if true, the traditional view of God's knowledge does not explain how God could know himself without a knowledge of the world. The most that the traditional theist can say is that in knowing himself, prior to the creation of the world, God has a knowledge of a possible not-self (cf. AW 11). But a merely possible world is not enough to ensure an actual self-knowledge. Once again, experience fails to provide the traditional theist with an adequate analogy. For it is a universal feature of experience that knowledge of possible states of affairs presupposes an acquaintance with the actual world. Unless God's self-knowledge is totally unlike our own, it too requires a world—a not-self—in terms of which the knowledge can occur. Rather than use words, the meaning of which we have no idea, God's self-knowledge should be conceived as the eminent form of what in us is called self-knowledge. The idea of God as knowing himself, then, entails the idea of some world or other.

The arguments thus far support Hartshorne's views that something or other necessarily exists and that, if God exists he does not exist without some world or other. Now, the impossibility of nonbeing at least shows that "Something exists" is necessary. Thus, the second lemma of the Hartshornean cosmological argument is already partially answered. Those who believe that what exists has no modal status must contend with the arguments thus far.[20] It might appear that by proving the necessary falsity of "Nothing exists" we have also proven that not everything is contingent. But this is false since the two statements "Everything that exists is contingent" and "Necessarily something exists" are subcontraries, not contradictories. There are many atheists who would agree to both propositions. Thus, the second half of the second lemma, "What exists is wholly contingent" must be argued.

Hartshorne suggests a line of reasoning similar to the traditional cosmological argument to defeat A2(b).

> . . . the necessity that at least something should exist is not intelligible apart from the idea of a being which exists necessarily (CS 283).

One way to read the argument is as follows: if everything is contingent then the universe is contingent. But, from the falsity of A1, the universe is not contingent. Therefore, not everything is contingent. According to Russell, the first premise of the argument involves a fallacy of composition. If the parts of the universe are contingent it does not follow that the universe as a whole is contingent.[21]

While it is true as a matter of general principle that the nature of the whole cannot be inferred from the nature of the parts, there are many cases in which whole and parts share a common characteristic. If each of the parts of a house is made of wood, then the house is made of wood. The claim of the premise in question is that there is no way many contingent things could be anything but contingent. This seems right, as John Shepherd points out:

> . . . if the constituents of the world are contingent the world itself must be so too, for contingency concerns the *existence* of things and the *existence* of the world is nothing over and above the existence of all its constituents. Thus, though a whole may possess some qualities which its parts do not, the nature of its existence cannot be different.[22]

The world, considered merely as a collection of contingent entities, cannot explain the necessity of existence. Only by reference to a necessary being is the world of contingent things made intelligible.

If Hartshorne's cosmological argument proved only that there is a necessary being, the case for theism would have been substantially strengthened. Whether the necessary being is also proved to have all or most of the attributes normally ascribed to God is of little importance as far as the cumulative case is concerned. To prove the existence of a necessary being is a long way toward proving the existence of

God. It is important, however, to demonstrate that there is more in the world than the necessarily existent. Philosophers of no small stature have explicitly denied the reality of contingency—Parmenides, Shankara, Spinoza, Bradley and Blanshard to mention only a few. Furthermore, Hartshorne's God has a contingent aspect. Indeed, the contingent is identified with the concrete. If God's existence and each aspect of his actuality were necessary, he would, according to Hartshornean principles, be only an abstraction. Thus, the falsity of A3—"What exists is wholly necessary"—is essential to Hartshorne's theism.

Common sense is almost certainly against the necessitarian. Contingency is felt as so pervasive an aspect of experience that to deny its reality seems to fly in the face of the most obvious of facts. For example, Alicia regrets her harsh words to Tamara. The regret implies she believes that she could have chosen her words more carefully. Furthermore, contingences are not simply referred to, they have genuine cognitive import. We can learn, in part, how to conduct our lives by thinking of what might have been. Any philosophy which requires that such a basic feature of existence is a mere appearance is, by the nature of the case, subject to suspicion. But the fact that brilliant minds have cast their votes against contingency is enough to take the philosophy seriously.

Hartshorne's favorite argument against necessitarianism is that it violates the principle of contrast (a similar argument applies to those who believe everything is contingent). The contrasts to which Hartshorne refers are such ultimate contraries as simple/complex, abstract/concrete, object/subject, cause/effect, etc. The necessary/contingent contrast is also part of the list. The principle of contrast is that,

> . . . the two poles of each contrast stand or fall together; neither is simply to be denied or explained away or called 'unreal'. For if either pole is real the contrast itself, including both poles, is so (CS 99).

In general philosophers do not question the principle of contrast. Where there is cause there is effect, where there is effect, cause. The simple is simple only as related to something which is not simple, the complex.[23] The claim is that the necessary/contingent distinction is no different. We have already seen how the concept of a contingent being implies the concept of a necessary being. Does the entailment hold the other way? According to the principle of contrast, the concept of necessity should imply the concept of contingency. Indeed, this is so. As Hartshorne notes,

A thing is necessary if no alternative to it is possible; but this presupposes a meaning and a referent for "possible" and for "alternative" which the doctrine that all things are necessary cannot provide (*PSG* 195).

In denying the reality of contingency, the necessitarian has denied a basis for the distinction between necessity and contingency. But since the necessary is *defined* in terms of the contingent (that is, that to which no alternative is possible), there must be a distinction. Other-wise, the concept of necessity is deprived of meaning.

Necessitarians do not usually deny the principle of contrast but try to account for the contrast between necessity and contingency by giving expressions such as "might have been otherwise," or "may be" an epistemic reading. After explaining his brand of Spinozism, Blanshard asks,

Does this mean that the language of "may" and "might" is meaningless? Not at all. It is perfectly legitimate, given the knowledge that we have, to say that it may rain tomorrow. But the statement is then about the extent of what we know.[24]

The contingent is, then, a function of our "invincible ignorance." If we could only see things, as a whole, or from the standpoint of om-niscience, it would be clear that what we thought was contingent, is really necessary.

The problem with Blanshard's argument is that an epistemic mean-ing of contingency is not enough to insure a genuine contrast with necessity. Blanshard can perhaps explain how we come to use the concept of contingency, but not how we can attach a clear meaning to necessity if contingency is not real. If, in the final analysis—or from the standpoint of omniscience—there is no contingency, then how is the notion of necessity meaningful? If everything is necessary there are no real alternatives or possibilities in terms of which necessity could be defined. Have we not reached the night in which all cows are black? This is not to say that notions involving contingency are not sometimes epistemic. But they are not merely epistemic. There is more to contingency than the concept of ignorance can exhaust. In-deed, ignorance itself is understandable only in terms of contingency. To be ignorant of something is to fail to know something that *could be* known.

Against necessitarianism, Hartshorne also points out that, apart from contingency, becoming is explained away (*CS* 283). Since this argument is developed in the next chapter we can leave the topic of necessitarianism and consider the view that there are both contingent and necessary things, but nothing is divine.

An argument for theism is not necessarily deficient if it fails to prove that the necessary being has all of the characteristics of God. Failure to prove X is not a proof of not-X. Other arguments may provide support for the belief that the necessary being is God. Nevertheless, there is a presumption in favor of the view that a necessary being must be divine. For it is not clear that anything but a divine being could be necessary. A nondivine being is, by definition, imperfect. But imperfection involves exclusiveness from other possibilities. For example, an imperfect knower is one to whom a certain amount of information is lacking; or again, an imperfect love is a love that fails to include the beloved totally. Similarly, imperfection of existence implies an exclusion, or cutting off of certain possibilities for being. A being which exists necessarily is, so far as the concept of existence is concerned, more perfect than a contingently existing being. Thus it seems likely that an imperfect, or nondivine being, could not exist necessarily.

Alvin Plantinga points out that necessary existence is one of several "great making" qualities. But a thing might exist necessarily without having any other great making qualities. In that case, the necessary being would not be divine.[25] What is at issue, however, is whether an imperfect being could have a great making quality. Could a non-divine being have a divine property?

In a sense, God and creatures must be conceived as sharing properties. Although a creature is an imperfect knower, it is a knower nonetheless. Creaturely power is limited, divine power is unlimited, but both are power. In another sense, however, being imperfect precludes having certain divine attributes. To be limited in space and time is to fail to be unlimited in knowledge. My death, for example, prevents me from knowing what happens afterwards. The same holds, *mutatis mutandis*, for the other divine attributes, omnipotence, omnipresence and omnibenevolence.

Could one be limited in knowledge, power or goodness and necessarily exist? There are certain deities, in religious literature, which fit this description. The evil deity of Zoroastrianism, Ahriman, is the best example. According to Zoroastrian mythology, Ohrmazd, the good deity, outwits and finally overpowers Ahriman in the final battle between good and evil. Although he necessarily exists, Ahriman is limited not only in goodness (he is the evil deity), but also in knowledge and power.[26] The question is whether something like Ahriman is genuinely conceivable.

If it is possible for a necessary being to be limited in knowledge, power, and goodness, then it is not a part of the essence of such a being to be omniscient, omnipotent and omnibenevolent. If the necessary being possesses these attributes at all, it is only accidentally. The theist must find this completely unacceptable. For God is, by hypothesis, a necessary being, but is not all-knowing, all-powerful or all-good merely by accident. These are *essential* properties of God. It follows that if there is a necessary being who is not essentially omnibenevolent, omnipotent and omniscient, that being cannot be God. The other elements of Hartshorne's global argument can be of help here. The design argument argues to a being whose essence is to exert universal influence (i.e., to be omnipotent); the epistemic argument concludes to the existence of an omniscient being; the moral and aesthetic arguments reason to a being who is wholly good and beautiful. If these arguments are successful then Hartshorne's claim that, "The necessary aspect of existence is . . . positively intelligible, if at all, only as the existence of deity" (CS 283-284), is true.

Hartshorne seems to think that the aid of the other arguments is not necessary to prove that the necessary being is divine. But I am not sure how this is possible. Whether it is possible or not to prove, without other arguments, that a necessary being is divine, is, in the context of the global argument irrelevant. For the other arguments *can* be used. This much Hartshorne would not deny. Let us, then, postpone the question of Ahriman's existence until we have examined Hartshorne's other arguments.

Due to the *a priori* nature of Hartshorne's cosmological argument, many criticisms aimed at traditional formulations of the argument simply miss the mark. Objections which rely on the assumption that the cosmological argument is an attempt to apply the principle of sufficient reason to the universe as a whole are irrelevant. Hartshorne makes no attempt to show why there is something rather than nothing. The assertion that something exists is, for Hartshorne, not empirical at all, but an *a priori* necessity. Furthermore, since there is no mention of the concept of cause, objections to a first-cause argument are also beside the point. Perhaps the only objection that is relevant is Kant's contention that the cosmological argument stands or falls with the ontological argument. With this, Hartshorne agrees. But Hartshorne does not have as low an opinion of the ontological argument as Kant. If Hartshorne's long career has accomplished nothing else, it has at least shown that the ontological argument is not as easily refuted as some have believed.

With these thoughts, let us leave the cosmological argument and consider the last in the famous triad of theistic proofs—the design argument.

VI
The Design Argument

The design argument for God's existence—or as it is sometimes called, the teleological argument—reasons either form the order of the universe as a whole or from particular examples of order within the universe to the existence of a divine ordering power. From its beginning in Plato, the argument, incorporating the many attacks of sceptics, reached a high level of sophistication in the writings of F. R. Tennant.[1] No one, however, in the argument's long history, ever understood the design argument as anything more than an empirical approach to God's existence, giving us at best good inductive or probabilistic grounds for believing in God. Hartshorne's version of the design argument is noteworthy if only because it purports to be, like the ontological proof, an *a priori* argument. In the context of the global argument, the design proof is meant to establish the conceivability of God by showing that any cosmic order requires a divine cosmic ordering power. Of course, if any cosmic order requires God, then, if there is a cosmic order, it follows not merely that God is conceivable but that God exists.

Hartshorne has discussed the design argument often. In *Man's Vision of God* (1941) the argument is considered only in its traditional empirical form and is rejected as inconsistent with the idea that God must be conceived as a necessary being (MVG 253). But as early as 1945 Hartshorne explicitly states the design argument in its *a priori* form (RSP 192). Perhaps the most comprehensive treatment of the argument is in A *Natural Theology for Our Time* (58–62). In *Creative Synthesis* (1970) the proof is incorporated as an element in the global argument (CS 281). The most recent treatments of the design argument were in 1972 and 1982.[2] Hartshorne is fond of presenting the design argument in terms of four alternatives, the last being the theistic alternative. The object is to show that only the theistic option is intelligible. The alternatives are as follows.

There is no cosmic order.
There is cosmic order but no cosmic ordering power.

> There is cosmic order and ordering power, but the power is
>   not divine.
> There is cosmic order and divine power.(CS 281).

The advantage of this formulation of the argument is that it makes explicit the price one must pay for rejecting theism. The argument is easily put into a more conventional form by transforming the first three alternatives into premises supporting the fourth alternative as the conclusion.

1.   There is cosmic order.
2.   If there is cosmic order there is a cosmic ordering power.
3.   If there is a cosmic ordering power then the power is divine.
4.   Therefore, there is a divine cosmic ordering power.

This version of the argument has the advantage of making explicit the positive claims for which Hartshorne must argue. The validity of the argument is also apparent from this formulation. From premises 2 and 3 it follows that cosmic order requires a divine ordering power. With the additional premise that there is cosmic order it follows that God, the divine cosmic ordering power, exists. All that remains to be seen is whether the premises are true.

The argument begins from the uncontroversial claim that there is cosmic order. Although chance, spontaneity, and novelty may play an important role in our understanding of nature, there is little doubt that the universe exhibits discoverable patterns and regularities. The point is not that disorder is nonexistent but that some degree of order is present throughout the universe. Thus, in claiming that there is cosmic order, Hartshorne is not committed to the further claim that the order is absolute, exceptionless, or perfect. Indeed, according to the metaphysics that Hartshorne adopts, any genuinely conceivable state of affairs involves elements of both regularity and irregularity.

Hartshorne's view is that an unordered universe is not genuinely conceivable. Traditional design arguments proceed on the assumption that the observable order in the world—or some aspect thereof—serves as the empirical premise of the argument. Tennant, a defender of the empirical design argument says,

> . . . the primary epistemological contribution to teleological
> reasoning consists in the fact the world is more or less intelli-
> gible, in that it happens to be more or less a cosmos, when

conceivably it might have been a self-subsistent and determinate 'chaos' in which similar events never occurred, none recurred, universals had no place, relations no fixity, things no nexus of determination, and 'real' categories no foothold.[3]

The premise that there is cosmic order is not empirical unless coherent meaning can be given to the idea of a purely disordered or chaotic universe. Normal usage of the concepts of disorder and chaos presupppose a minimal amount of order. For example, the furniture in a warehouse may exhibit no purposive arrangement and so we say the furniture is not ordered. But there is at least enough order for there to be furniture and a warehouse. Or again, a scientist may speak poetically of the meaningless, chaotic collision of atoms. Once again, there must be at least an atomic order, that is, enough order to maintian atoms in existence. When Tennant speaks of things having "no nexus of determination," or of 'real' categories having no foothold, it is not clear that he is speaking of anything that could be conceived.

The argument from the ordinary usage of words like order and disorder casts serious doubt on the possibility of a completely unordered universe. But Hartshorne prefers another argument. According to neoclassical metaphysics, to be knowable and to be are the same. Hartshorne would agree with Peirce who says,

> Over against any cognition, there is an unknown but knowable reality; but over against all possible cognition, there is only the self-contradictory. In short, *cognizability* (in its widest sense) and *being* are not merely metaphysically the same, but are synonymous terms.[4]

If Peirce is correct, and if a chaotic universe is unknowable then it could not exist. But, as Hartshorne notes, an absolutely unordered universe would be absolutely unknowable since no knowledge could exist in it (CS 284). In this respect, a chaotic world is indistinguishable from nonbeing since neither could, in principle, be known. Against this view, one could argue that the *possibility* of a chaotic universe is knowable even though it (the chaotic universe) would be unknowable by anything existing within it. Hartshorne would counter this suggestion by asking what distinguishes a knowledge of the possibility of a chaotic universe from knowledge of the possibility of nonbeing. Since no one ever has, or could have experienced either one, it is not clear how a distinction could be made. Indeed, Hartshorne maintains that nonbeing *is* indistinguishable from pure chaos (CS 284). But, as the discussion of the cosmological argument makes clear, philosophers have failed to give coherent sense to the idea of nonbeing. Thus, if chaos is indistinguishable from nonbeing it shares the same fate; and we may safely assume that neither concept corresponds to anything that is or could be. The arguments examined thus far point in this direction.

Let us now move to the second premise, which seems most in need of justification. Hartshorne claims that cosmic order requires a cosmic ordering power. The burden of proof is on Hartshorne to justify this claim since there are many examples of order which do not require an ordering power. Stalactites and stalagmites are always ordered in such a way that one is directly above the other.[5] Yet no one believes that this order requires an ordering power. The order of the universe may be of a similar nature. Hartshorne must give grounds for thinking that the order of the universe, unlike other kinds of order, requires an ordering power. This brings us to the heart of Hartshorne's proof. Hartshorne's design argument rests on a certain view of reality—of what it means to be real. Let us first examine the logic of the design argument without questioning the truth of Hartshorne's creationist philosophy. We may then turn a critical eye to the Hartshornean metaphysic.

The cornerstone of Hartshorne's design argument is the claim that the order of nature is an instance of social order, that is, order among a variety of partly free individuals. The individuals in this case are the ultimate constituents of reality, what Whitehead calls actual entities and what Hartshorne sometimes calls dynamic singulars. Every actual entity is a partly self-creative process of bringing the welter of data from its past into a determinate unity. Whitehead refers to this process as 'concrescence' to suggest that it is the 'becoming concrete' of a new actual entity. Once the process of concrescence is complete, the actual entity becomes a datum for subsequent actual entities. Whitehead says that the many become one and are increased by the one.

Although the actual entity emerges from the past, it is not totally determined by its past. An actual entity is partly self-creative, that is to say, partly free. In Hartshorne's words, "To be is to create." (CS 1). If the actual entity is not wholly determined by its past, neither is it wholly free. The freedom of an actual entity always occurs within the limitations set by the becoming of past actual entities. The past conditions, if it does not completely determine, the present concrescence.

Since the conditions, or limitations, set for an actual entity come from past actual entities, the limits to freedom are other acts of freedom. (CS 7). Previous acts of freedom (i.e., actual entities) define the backdrop within which the present act of freedom occurs. The present actual entity is an emergent synthesis from the past.

To speak of the limits to freedom is another way of speaking of order. The limitations to creativity are the measure of order in the world. Since Hartshorne is not a strict determinist, he does not believe the order is absolute. Nevertheless, that there is a large degree of order in the world is undeniable. The important point is that Hartshorne explains the order in the world as the result of acts of freedom (actual entities) setting limits to subsequent acts of freedom.

The nerve of Hartshorne's design argument is that only "divine acts of cosmic relevance" can adequately account for order on a cosmic scale (CS 9). If there were no individual inclusive of the universe then there would be no explanation of cosmic order. Hartshorne says,

> Thus, in the reasonable argument from design, we may argue that if all interaction is supposed to be local and more or less unknowing, it is not to be understood how reality could be or remain anything but a "shapeless chaos"—to quote Jefferson's phrase, used in this connection. Only universal interaction can secure universal order, or impose and maintain laws of nature cosmic in scope and relevant to the past history of the universe. (NT 53).

Hartshorne says elsewhere, "the axiom here is that plurality of agents amounts, in the absence of a supreme agent, to chaos." (RSP 92).

One should not suppose that because Hartshorne speaks of an alternative between the existence of a cosmic ordering power and "shapeless chaos" that he assumes that a completely unordered universe is possible. As we have already seen, Hartshorne does not believe cosmic chaos is genuinely conceivable. Not even God, says Hartshorne, has "the choice between world-order and chaos." (WP 133). Thus, it cannot be said that God rescues the world from chaotic nonbeing since there is no possibility of complete chaos. Nevertheless, God is necessary to explain the cosmic order since no nondivine individual or group of individuals could secure this order. Local interaction, that is, the interaction between nondivine individuals, could only result in a local, not a cosmic order.

Without calling the creationist philosophy itself into question, the only alternative to the idea of a supreme ordering power, is the idea of mutual adjustment. If more than one ordering power is assumed, none having universal influence, then the only explanation of cosmic order that could be given is in terms of the mutual adjustment of free agents. Hartshorne rejects an explanation of order in terms of mutual adjustment as question-begging.

> If all individuals make their own decision, act with a certain spontaneity, what prevents universal conflict and confusion? Can all things freely conspire together to make an orderly world? Each adjusts to all the others; but one cannot adjust to chaos. Hence the notion of "mutual adjustment" presupposes the solution of the problem of order, and does not furnish it. (WP 133).

Once again, one may be misled by Hartshorne's reference to chaos into thinking that the argument presupposes the conceivabililty of a purely chaotic universe. But this is not the case. Hartshorne's point is that the idea of mutual adjustment, *on a cosmic scale*, presupposes at least a minimal amount of cosmic order. If there are individuals adjusting to each other to create order there must be at least enough order for the individuals to exist. But if we consider mutual adjustment on a cosmic scale, there must be a cosmic order to allow for this adjustment. The idea of mutual adjustment presupposes a relatively stable context within which the adjustment can occur. Thus, cosmic mutual adjustment presupposes cosmic order.

One might grant Hartshorne his metaphysic of creativity but question the need for a cosmic ordering power to explain cosmic order. According to Hartshorne's view, only contingent truths require explanation. A necessary truth is its own explanation—it *could not* be otherwise. But, as we have seen Hartshorne believes that the existence of cosmic order is a necessary truth. Why should cosmic order require any further explanation? This criticism rests on an ambiguity in the idea of cosmic order. According to Hartshorne, the existence and order of the world is no accident. It is necessarily true that there is an orderly universe. But Hartshorne denies that any particular instance of cosmic order is necessary (RSP 51). The laws of nature are contingent, but it is not contingent that there are natural laws (AD 186). What God is required to explain is not the ncesssary truth that there is some form of cosmic order; rather, God's ordering power explains the particular cosmic order that happens to exist.

> I personally take the laws of nature as the chief identifiable aspects of God's creative action. So far as the laws are contin-

gent, they imply divine creativity, and I agree with Aristotle that nothing eternal is contingent, hence no law is eternal unless it is without possible alternative.[6]

Just as God has both necessary and contingent aspects—God's existence is necesary, his actuality is contingent—so the order of nature is both necessary and contingent. The laws of nature, according to Hartshorne, change; but it is necessary that there are natural laws.

The internal logic of Hartshorne's creationist metaphysic, according to which the universe is composed of a variety of partly free or self-creative individuals, demands that there be one individual whose influence has cosmic scope. Since the limits to freedom are the measure of the order in the world, cosmic order requires a cosmic ordering power. But what reason is there to believe that the universe is full of free creatures? The immediate evidence of the senses seems to dictate the opposite conclusion. The universe is full of inert, dead, and inactive stuff. Furthermore, even in those areas of nature in which there is activity, one may question the propriety of labeling that activity free, or of speaking of the individuals involved as self-creative. In what sense, for example, is the activity of the pumping of a heart free? The point is that if the creationist metaphysic is either false or meaningless, then Hartshorne's design argument cannot be employed as an element of his cumulative case.

Although a full treatment of a creationist philosophy is impossible within the confines of this work, a few remarks should be offered in its defense. Like Whitehead, Hartshorne takes creativity to be the most generic feature of existence. In Whitehead's words,

> 'Creativity' is the universal of universals characterizing ultimate matter of fact. It is that ultimate principle by which the many, which are the universe disjunctively, become the one actual occasion, which is the universe conjunctively. It lies in the nature of things that the many enter into complex unity.[7]

Every ultimately real thing—every actual entity—is an instance of creativity. "The many become one and are increased by the one."[8] As already noted, process philosophers (like Whitehead and Hartshorne) believe becoming is more basic than being. Hartshorne's argument for this view is that the concept of becoming is more inclusive that the concept of being.

> Becoming or process can be so conceived that it entirely
> includes its own contrast with being, while being cannot be
> conceived to include its contrast with becoming. More pre-
> cisely: What becomes and what does not become (but simply
> is) together constitute a total reality which becomes.[9]

Hartshorne is not saying that becoming can exist without being, for wherever there is process or change, there is that which is unchanging. Hartshorne agrees with Aristotle that "all change requires something changing that does not come to exist through that same change." (MVG 233). In this sense, becoming and being are equally real.

Philosophers of being sometimes argue that since an unchanging reality can exist independent of change, the unchanging reality (being) must be ontologically more basic. For example, a person remains self-identical through a variety of changes—the self-identical 'being' exists independent of these changes. But this argument rests on an ambiguity in the idea of independence. The color red exists independent of its particular instantiations. But it does not follow that red exists independent of *all* instantiations. Similarly, a man retains his self-identity through many changes. But who has shown that the man can exist independent of all changes? Hartshorne and other process philosophers admit that being is independent of any particular change but deny that being is independent of all change. One of the chief merits of process philosophy is that it affirms the contrast between being and becoming without reducing either side of the contrast to a mere appearance, illusion, or accidental reality. For Hartshorne neither process nor being is accidentally real. Both are essential, although being is an abstraction from a reality that becomes. For Hartshorne, the distinction between being and becoming corresponds to the distinction between the abstract and the concrete. Both the abstract and the concrete are real, but just as the abstract is an aspect of the concrete, being is an aspect of becoming.

The fact that nature, in its grosser features, exhibits an apparent lack of activity in no way detracts from the view that the most concrete entities are units of becoming. The proper conclusion is that objects such as rocks and planets are not the most concrete entities. Hartshorne's view is that inanimate objects are collections or groupings (called 'societies') of the more concrete actual entities. This conclusion is supported by empirical considerations. The inactivity of a rock, as a whole, tends to conceal the fact that its molecular constituents are in constant motion. Surrounded on every side by inert material objects,

it is easy to forget that beneath the veil of inactivity is a hidden world—
that is, a world hidden from our unaided senses—of bustling restlessness. Nature is forever changing, however static at any moment it
may appear. Evolutionary theories in biology and astronomy also support this view. Stars and galaxies are constantly being born or dying;
and the biosphere is an arena of the birth and death of species. The
universe is in flux, far from the static whole envisaged by some of our
ancestors.

This restlessness of nature is nowhere better exemplified than in
human beings. According to Hartshorne, the knowledge we have of
our own emotional and bodily activity provides a direct insight into
a fundamental truth about the nature of things. Although it is clear
that consciousness is restricted to higher forms of animal life, it seems
equally clear that the dynamism characterizing so much of nature is
shared by conscious beings. Hartshorne maintains that the activity
found in atoms, molecules, cells, or lower life forms is manifested in
eminent form in human consciousness. Thus, the freedom and creativity in humans is found in lesser degrees in other creatures. This is
not to say that, for example, a molecule is creative in exactly the same
sense as a human being. There are greater and lesser degrees of creativity.

> And this phrase "creative activity," or "creative becoming,"
> only escapes redundancy because there are degrees of creativity,
> implying the zero case as lower limit of thought, a necessarily
> fictitious entity, like "perfect lever," or "wholly isolated
> particle." (*LP* 166).

Some might object that talk of creativity or freedom in subhuman
creatures is an unwarranted anthropomorphism. But such an objection
reveals too narrow a conception of psychological predicates. As Hartshorne remarks, "They betray themselves by their reiterated charge that
to psychologize everything is to humanize everything—as if an animal
caught in a trap must become a man to suffer." (*BH* 120). Attributing
a minimal amount of freedom to subhuman individuals does not, therefore, warrant the charge of anthropomorphism. Indeed, if, as Hartshorne claims, the ideas of freedom and creativity have "an unlimited
breadth or flexibility (*BH* 119), then there would be no apparent
reason why all individuals could not, in some measure, however slight,
be free. Both Hartshorne's metaphysical argument for the foundational
nature of becoming and empirical considerations lend support to this
creationist philosophy.

The argument thus far supports the claim that cosmic order requires a cosmic ordering power. It has yet to be shown that the cosmic ordering power (COP) is divine, that is, that the ordering power has all of the attributes normally ascribed to God. If the entire burden of proving theism rested on the design argument, this deficiency would be a serious obstacle to finding a rational basis for theistic belief. But we have already seen that several arguments may be used to prove God's existence. Nevertheless, Hartshorne offers a reason for believing that the COP is divine.

> We have some insight in experience into the power of agents over other agents. A man as conscious being sways his bodily constituents (cells, etc.). He is incomparably the most powerful agent in his psychophysical system. He is also, we all in effect assume, incomparably the most important and valuable. His experience sums up what is going on in the system vastly more than any events involved in the other agents, taken individually. By analogy we conceive the cosmic ordering power as the supreme or eminent form of awareness. (CS 284–285).

Hartshorne's point is that the best analogy in human experience for conceiving the relationship between COP and individuals within the cosmos is the mind-body relation. The cosmic orderer is related to individuals within the cosmos as the human mind is related to the human body. But, just as the mind is superior to its bodily parts in knowledge, worth, and power, so the cosmic orderer is superior to individuals in the cosmos.

The analogy with the human body is incomplete and in some respects misleading if understood too literally. The purpose of the analogy is to isolate certain features of the mind-body relation which might apply to the COP-world relation. We are not to believe, for example, that the universe has arms, legs, muscles, bones, nerves, or blood vessels. Nevertheless, the power the mind has over its bodily constituents is similar to the power the COP has over worldly constituents. To be sure, the mind is not responsible for all of the order within the body—although recent work with biofeedback techniques have demonstrated that the mind is (or can be) responsible for more than was hitherto believed. We can say, however, that the mind exerts more control than any single member of the bodily complex and is therefore the most powerful member of the psychophysical system. Further, one may speculate that any bodily order for which the mind is not responsible is due to factors pertaining to the body's external environment, a feature not shared by the COP's 'body'. The human body is, after all, part of the larger ordered whole which is the universe. But, as Hartshorne notes, there is no environment external to the universe (*NT* 98). This fact may explain why the cosmic 'body', unlike its creaturely counterparts, does not undergo decay and dissolution.

> To have an external environment is to depend upon factors
> not under immediate control, and sooner or later these factors
> may happen to conflict fatally with one's internal needs.
> But the universe as a whole, if it is an organism at all, must
> immediately control all its parts; so what is to prevent it
> from setting unsurpassable limits to disintegration in relation
> to construction? (*MVG* 181).

It is reasonable to assume that the death of the human body is the inevitable result of the body being only a part, or a fragment of the universe, and that the body depends upon things for its existence. To be dependent for one's existence on external conditions is to be subject to death. But the universe cannot be dependent in the way a human body is dependent. Thus, the analogy with a human body breaks down at this point for good reasons.

If, as many scientists believe, the second law of thermodynamics is applicable to the universe as a whole there may be some analogy between the decay of the human body and the dissolution of the universe. According to Hartshorne, the universe cannot cease to exist. It may, however, lose its present form and acquire another. As noted above, Hartshorne holds that the laws of nature are contingent, but that it is not contingent that there are natural laws. It may be that the universe, as we know it, is 'running down', that is increasing in entropy. What will happen when the process is complete is not known. But if Hartshorne (following Whitehead) is correct, the present universe will eventually be superseded by a new cosmic epoch with laws of its own. One reason for the succession of cosmic epochs is aesthetic. Beauty requires both unity and contrast, similarity and difference. If the universe as a whole is beautiful then an element of contrast is required; "eventually the repetitions of the patterns disclosed by current physics would call for relief from monotony in new patterns." (*RSP* 50). The claim that the universe as a whole is beautiful is supported in chapter IX. Suffice it to say that the theory of cosmic epochs is not an arbitrary addition to Harshorne's metaphysics.

An important consequence of Hartshorne's analogy is that God cannot remain unaffected by what happens in the universe. What occurs in the human body influences the mind. Similarly, God is influenced by what happens in the universe. Traditionally, theists have followed Aristotle in the idea that God is immutable. We have seen, however, that God, neoclassically conceived, is not immutable. Thus, Hartshorne is able to accommodate (and welcomes) this consequence of the analogy. Creaturely decisions have a real affect on the divine life.

Before closing, it would be instructive to survey the major objections to the design argument and see what, if any, force they have against Hartshorne's version of the argument. Some objections have already been covered. Hume's queries of why the natural order requires explanation and why, if it does require explanation, it is to be explained by reference to God have been addressed. The natural order is an instance of social order and thus requires explanation. And the cosmic ordering power is best conceived as a cosmic mind exerting influence over its 'bodily' constituents. Other objections have been given implicit replies. For example, to the question of why the designer's mind is not as much in need of explanation as the world he designs, it can be replied that the order of God's mind is self-imposed and is thus not an instance of social order (*RSP* 192). Or again, some critics claim that an experience of several universes is a prerequisite to knowing that the order of our own universe points to an intelligent designer. But we only have experience of one universe. Hartshorne's claim, however, is that any conceivable universe requires an intelligent designer. The argument is not inductive, it is a *a priori*. The only serious objection that has not been covered is the problem of evil.

Prima facie, the existence of evil in the world argues against the existence of a good designer. On occasion, Hartshorne has admitted that evil may be a formidable barrier to theistic belief (*OD* 239, *MVG* 195). In his own words, "A partially botched product can hardly be sufficient evidence for a perfect producer." (*NT* 58). At times, however, Hartshorne is less kind to the critic who takes evil as a disproof of God's existence. He labels the traditional problem of evil a piece of "semantic jugglery" (*CS* 293). Hartshorne is confident that, once the problem is understood, the existence of evil poses no serious threat to theism. Yet, even if it can be shown that the problem of evil is semantic jugglery, strictly speaking, such a demonstration is not essential to the defense of the design argument. The design argument may be construed, in the context of a cumulative case, only as an attempt to prove the existence of an intelligent designer. There is absolutely no obligation, as far as the design argument is concerned, to prove that the designer is supremely good. The goodness of God can perhaps be proved through other arguments of the cumulative case. As far as Hartshorne's global argument is concerned, the moral argument is directly relevant to God's goodness.

A convincing argument can be made, however, that the cosmic ordering power could not be evil. We have already seen that if God is related to the world as the mind is related to the body, then, just as the mind is thought to be more valuable than any part of the body, so God must be considered more valuable than any part of the world.

The mind-body analogy raises another consideration. If the world is construed as the divine body then God could inflict suffering on his creatures only by doing harm to himself. God could be a sadist only if he were also a masochist. Hartshorne makes the point as follows.

> The cosmos could not be held together and ordered by malevolence, which as Plato argued, is always partly divided against itself and is also incapable of an objective grasp of reality; but the cosmos could be held together by an all-sympathetic co-ordinator, a shepherd of all beings. (RSP 190).

Evil is a destructive agency which occasions disorder rather than order. "Evil does not require cosmic coordiation, for it is essentially anarchic, egocentric or ethnocentric."[10] An evil deity could only tend to undermine the very thing that needs explaining, namely, cosmic order.

Persons who have followed the design argument to the point of believing that there is a cosmic ordering power may agree that demonic attributes do not belong to that power. They may insist, however, that the cosmic orderer is not good. In other words, the cosmic ordering power is viewed as morally neutral with respect to the things he orders. The problem of evil, then, is not understood as a refutation of the existence of a cosmic designer; rather, it is taken as a proof that the designer is not God. Again, the reader is reminded that Hartshorne's design argument is only one element in a cumulative case. There are considerations, extraneous to the design argument proper, which support the goodness of God. Nevertheless, an overview of Hartshorne's theodicy may serve to highlight our discussion of the design argument. We may better understand how the disorder which is evil is related to the order of the world.

The several ways of stating the problem of evil can be reduced to two, which I call the incompatibility thesis and the improbability thesis: 1) The existence of evil is incompatible with the existence of a good God, and 2) The enormous amount of apparently unjustified evil in the world makes the existence of a good God improbable. J. L. Mackie, H. J. McCloskey, and Antony Flew argue for the incompatibility thesis. Edward Madden, Peter Hare, and Peter Hutcheson argue for the improbability thesis.[11]

The incompatibility thesis is effectively refuted by an appeal to creaturely freedom. Theologically speaking, the significance of human freedom is that it makes a genuine relationship with God and other creatures (human and nonhuman) possible. Without freedom, the creature is a mere puppet in the hands of the creator, incapable of creative response. But the same freedom which allows for loving relationships equally allows for rejection, hatred, and moral depravity. Evil can be explained as the inevitable result of freedom. Hartshorne says, "Risk of evil and opportunity for good are two aspects of just one thing, multiple freedom. . . . " (NT 81). The contention that God could have created free creatures who always choose the good is simply false.[12] A careful analysis reveals that an open future, that is, a future with genuine alternatives is a necessary condition of freedom.[13] But as noted in Chapter III, detailed knowledge of an indeterminate future is logically impossible. Thus, God could not know, in advance, what decisions a free creataure would make; that is, God could not be in a position to guarantee that every decision will be good.

The logic of the idea of freedom applies not alone to human freedom. Hartshorne notes that,

> Illness may be caused by all sorts of agents other than God, including bacteria . . . Decision-making, which is the essence of power, cannot in its broadest meaning be confined to God, nor even to God and man, no, not even to God and the animals. Rather it pervades reality generally.[14]

We have touched again on Hartshorne's philosophy of universal creativity. If this view of reality is correct then the traditional notion of an omnipotent being as someone capable of guaranteeing the results of creaturely decisions must be abandoned. Without the traditional concept of omnipotence, the incompatibility thesis loses its force.

The improbability thesis is more subtle than the incompatibililty thesis but is no less mistaken in its assumptions. According to the improbabililty thesis, the enormous amount of apparently unjustified suffering in the world makes the existence of a good God improbable.

The two important assumptions on which this claim rests are (a) that any instance of unjustified suffering is incompatible with the existence of a good God and (b) the question of God's existence can be decided solely on empirical grounds. Hartshorne takes issue with both assumptions.

The notion of an unjustified evil is not clear. As Hartshorne points out, "Any evil has some value from some perspective, for even to know it exists is to make it contributory to a good, knowledge itself being a good." (NT 80). If an unjustified evil is understood as any instance of suffering for which no ultimate reason can be given, then it must be admitted that there are many unjustified evils.

> If anyone asks for some profound reason why just his friend, or his child, or he himself, should die prematurely, I can only say, this is how the chances came out. Life simply is a gamble, and there is no remedy for that.[15]

To insist that every instance of suffering must contribute to a perfect whole if God exists is to deny the reality of chance. In the words of Emerson, it is to insist that "The dice of God are always loaded."[16] Hartshorne will have no part of a chanceless universe. It is in the nature of things that events do not always turn out for the best.

> If X decides to perform act A and Y decides to perform act B, what occurs is the conjunction of the two acts, A and B. But this conjuction neither agent has decided. It has just happened, so far as either's decision is concerned. Suppose for X we substitute God. The logic remains: God decides A, and not God but God *and* Y decide A *and* B. Since there are many decision makers, what happens is always something no one, not even God, has decided.[17]

Despite the reality of chance, the neoclassical God is able to make the best of the decisions individuals in the world have made.

> God can take each successive phase of the cosmic development and make unsurpassably good use of that phase (a) in his own life, and (b) in furnishing the creatures with such guidance or inspiration (their "initial subjective aims") as (my formula) will optimize the ratio of opportunities and risks for the next phase.[18]

One may still ask—like Madden and Hare—why there is so much unjustified suffering. Couldn't God at least prevent some of the evil in the world and thus make the world a better place? The obvious response to such a query is: how do you know he doesn't?[19] On what grounds does the critic claim to know that God does not prevent as much evil as he could without depriving nondivine individuals of their freedom? As we have seen, the neoclassical God is responsible for the framework within which freedom operates, namely, the laws of nature. And according to Hartshorne,

> The ideal rule [God's] sets those limits outside of which free-
> dom would involve greater risks than opportunities. Risks
> cannot be banished, for opportunity would go with them, both
> having the same root in freedom or self-determination. But
> too much freedom would extend risks more than opportunities,
> and too little would restrict opportunities more than risks.
> (LP 321).

There is admittedly a great deal of evil in the world. This is to be expected given the reality of creaturely freedom. But how much is too much? God would be in a position to answer this question but it is not clear any nondivine individual could provide the answer—at least through empirical evidence. This brings us to the second assumption of the improbability thesis, namely, that the existence of God is to be decided empirically.

Alvin Plantinga argues that none of the major theories of probability provide the critic with an adequate basis on which to build an argument against God's existence.[20] Hartshorne would agree, but on grounds different from those offered by Plantinga. According to Hartshorne, Anselm's great discovery was that the question of God's existence is not an empirical issue.[21] As noted in chapter IV, a minimal require-ment for a statement to count as empirical is that it is falsifiable by some conceivable experience. We can add here that verifiability by some conceivable experience is a necesary condition of empiricality (indeed, verifiability seems to be a necessary condition of coherent meaningfulness). But, we have argued—in the discussion of the on-tological argument—that God either exists in every possible world or in no possible world. It follows that, if God does not exist, this ex-istence is unverifiable; and the statement that he does (or does not) exist is not empirical. But if God does exist, his existence is unfalsi-fiable; and the statement that he does (or does not) exist is not empirical. Whether God exists or not, the issue is not empirical. The assumption of the improbability thesis, however, is that God's existence is an empirical question. The enormous amount of apparently unjustified suffering is offered as empirical evidence that a good God does not exist. An examination of the logic of the concept of God demonstrates the futility of digging around in empirical facts to find the presence or absence of the divine. The improbability thesis is therefore not a convincing argument against theism.

Hartshorne's design argument escapes the major criticisms against traditional formulations of the argument. This is in part because it is nonempirical and because it is a part of a cumulative case. Any problems the argument may have are probably unique to this version. The status and possibility of nonempirical arguments and the creationist view of nature are obvious points at which the argument may either be attacked or further supported by future inquiry. For our part, we leave the argument to consider other elements of Hartshorne's cumulative case.

VII
The Epistemic Argument

The first of the normative arguments for God's existence is called epistemic or idealistic. Compared to other arguments for God's existence, the epistemic proof has a short history in philosophical literature. Although St. Augustine argued for the existence of God from eternal truths, his argument differs in important respects from what we refer to here as the epistemic argument. The epistemic proof argues for divine existence not from eternal truths but form the concept of reality. The argument is suggested in Kant's distinction between phenomena and noumena (PSG 143). Later, Royce developed the Kantian suggestion into an argument for his own version of pantheism (PSG 198–201). Hartshorne revises the Roycean argument by correcting what he sees as defects in traditional versions of Idealism. As with most other elements of Hartshorne's philosophy, the epistemic argument first appears in rather attenuated form in his dissertation (OD 203). More lengthy and detailed discussions appeared in 1946, 1953 and 1967.[1] *Creative Synthesis* (1970) contains the first formal statement of the epistemic argument (CS 286).

The argument is stated as follows:

A1   Reality (or truth) is in no way dependent upon knowledge.
A2   Reality is actual or potential content of nondivine knowledge.
A3   Reality is potential content of divine knowledge (what God would know if he existed).
T   Reality is actual content of divine knowledge. (CS 286).

Summarily, the argument is that the concept of reality is meaningless when divorced from the concept of knowledge or experience. But the only idea of knowledge adequate to clarify the concept of reality is divine knowledge. Thus, the concept of reality implies the concept of God: to be real is to be the content of an infallible awareness.

95

An alternative Hartshorne does not consider is the position that there is no reality, or nothing is real. If there were nothing real, there would be no content of infallible awareness and God's existence could not be proved. We have already seen, however, in connection with the cosmological and design arguments, that Hartshorne rejects this position. "Something exists" entails "Something is real." If the former is, as Hartshorne argues, a necessary truth, then, since a necessary truth can only imply other necessary truths, "Something is real" must also be necessarily true.

If something is real, how are we to define the real? In agreement with the Idealist tradition, Hartshorne argues that reality cannot be understood apart from knowledge or experience. The most illustrious defender of the opposite view is Kant who maintained a sharp division between phenomena and noumena, the latter of which is real but beyond experience.[2] But Kant's position is subtle and it is not clear that he can be put decisively in a camp opposing the Idealist tradition. Phenomena are things, as they appear to us, through the forms of sensibility and the categories of the understanding. Noumena are the things, as they exist in themselves. Kant suggests that noumenal reality is knowable only by a nonsensory intuition. The problem is that Kant refuses to believe that we have a clear idea of nonsensory intuition (and this is one reason he would reject the epistemic proof). Thus, we don't know what it would mean to know things-in-themselves. There is no clear sense, then, on Kantian grounds, in saying that noumena are knowable.

The problem with the Kantian position, or anything similar to it, is that we are deprived of any reason we might have had for believing in an unknowable reality by the supposition that it is unknowable. If evidence is, by definition, unable to establish the existence or truth of x, then there could be no reason to believe in x. This is a major problem in Kant's philosophy. If knowledge is possible only through the forms of sensibility and the categories of the understanding, then on what grounds does Kant assert the existence of the noumena? As we have seen, Kant rejected the one answer he might have given to this question, namely, that we could know that a nonsensory intuition could know the noumenal reality.

Royce makes a persuasive case that reality is agreement between concepts and percepts.

> To question means to have ideas of what is not now present, and to ask whether these ideas do express, or could express,

what some experience could verify. (PSG 198).

Questions about what is real invariably refer to some verifying or fal-sifying experience. Hartshorne says,

> We compare ideas with perceived segments of reality, not with unperceived segments. If then reality is that which ideas are tested by, only experienced reality counts. Concepts are found true when they square with percepts, not with mere things in themselves. This is what all science in practice assumes and must assume.[3]

An engineer wishes to know whether a certain formula correctly de-scribes the fluid flow through a porous medium. Through experiment and observation—in short, through experience—the question is an-swered. The Roycean argument also seems to apply to nonempirical questions. A logician may wonder whether, given a set of axioms, a certain theorem is derivable. This can only mean that, given enough time and adequate care in reasoning, it will either be verified or falisifed that the theorem is derivable (We will discuss nonempirical quesitons more thoroughly a bit later.).

Summing up the argument, Hartshsorne says,

> Given truth we can define reality, or given reality we can define truth (Tarski's definition assumes the difference between real and imaginary 'grass'), but to define either apart from some notion of evidence is impossible. (CS 287).

The reference to Tarski should not be taken as a criticism of Tarski's definition of truth. It is simply a reminder that Tarski's work in no way decides the question of the connection between reality and ex-perience, a point with which Tarski would agree.[4]

It is important to clarify what, in the final analysis, Hartshorne means by saying that reality depends upon knowledge. In *Reality as Social Process* he distinguishes the principle of Objective Independence from the principal of Universal Objectivity (RSP 70). Objective In-dependence refers to the belief that the object of awareness or knowl-edge in no way depends upon the subject. For example, the red pencil before me is independent of my awareness. When I leave the room the pencil does not vanish. Universal Objectivity refers to the belief that "any entity must be (or at least be destined to become) object for *some* subject or other." (RSP 70). The principle of Universal Objectivity explains the sense in which Hartshorne believes reality depends on knowledge. The principle of Objective Independence explains the sense in which reality is not dependent on knowledge. The pencil is independent of my awareness or the awareness of any other particular subject (Objective Independence). But, the pencil is not independent of some awareness or other (Universal Objectivity). It is necessary that the pencil be known, but it is not necessary that the pencil be known by me, or any other particular subject.

Concerning the compatibility of these principles Hartshorne says,

> There is no contradiction in combining these assumptions; just as no logical difficulty opposes combining, "John must wear some garment rather than none" with "There is no necessity for John to wear this coat" (rather than some other garment). (RSP 71).

There is no logical bridge from the belief that reality depends upon knowledge to the belief that the objects of awareness are generated by or ontologically dependent on any particular knower. "Reality depends upon being known by *some* knower or knowers, but not upon just what particular knowers fulfill this requirement."[5]

One may argue that the principle of Objective Independence breaks down if God exists. For no object could be independent of an infallible awareness. If theism is true, does not the pencil depend upon one particular knower, namely, God? Hartshorne denies that God is a particular knower in any sense that would make the principle of Objective Independence false. It is true that an object is never indepenent of God's knowledge. But, to say God knows an object is to leave unspecified the particular way in which the object is known.

> . . . the fact that God knows us is far from a complete description of God's actual concrete knowing of us. There is the question of how he knows us, in what perspective he puts this knowledge, with what valuational nuances, etc.[6]

Hartshorne denies that there is only one way in which God could be aware of any given object. "There is never only one possible perfect solution to the problems the world poses for God."[7] There are alternatives even for God. This is not to say that God is free to choose the evil. For whatever decision God makes, it is unsurpassably good. "'God is good' means that he cannot choose between better and worse but only between actions all unsurpassably good . . . ."[8] Returning to the pencil example, if a_1, a_2 . . . a^n represent the possible ways God could know the pencil, we can say that the pencil remains itself whether God knows it in manner a_1, a_2 or a^n. But the pencil is not independent of the fact that God knows it in some way or other. Assuming the existence of a God whose knowledge has an element of contingency, the principle of Objective Independence is not violated.

One can deny the principle of Universal Objectivity and still believe there is a sense in which reality depends on knowledge. This is evident when we look at A2: Realilty is actual or potential content of non-divine knowlege. One might agree that 'being' and 'knowability' are coextensive (or synonymous) but insist that to be real is only to be the potential, not the actual object of knowledge—let us call this the K-thesis. The K-thesis is different from Hartshorne's principle of Universal Objectivity which says that everything is, *or will become*, an object of awareness. It is not unusual to believe, if one is not a theist, that many events have occurred, or will occur, without ever being known. This belief is consistent with the claim that the existence of such events consists in their abililty to be known. This is just to say that, *if* a subject were situated properly, the event in question would become an object of knowledge. But there is no necessity, if God does not exist, that there always be a subject who is actually aware of the event.

The K-thesis is essentially an attempt to define reality in terms of nondivine capacity for experience. The real is what is, or might be, the object of a nondivine awareness. Hartshorne rejects the K-thesis for at least three reasons, (1) the K-thesis involves a paradoxical shift from *is* to *might be*, (2) there are limits to nondivine capacity for clarity, and (3) there are things that no merely nondivine knowledge could know. Let us look at each of these arguments separately.

To my knowledge, Hartshorne has used the argument that the K-thesis is paradoxical in only place in his published work. He says,

> . . . to define reality as how things *would* appear to us if we were clear and certain is to define the *is* in terms of the *might be*, and this shift of modality is a paradox, if not a downright contradiction.[9]

Presumably what Hartshorne has in mind is that reality cannot be defined as something that *might be* since, by definition, reality is something that is. I do not find this argument very convincing. The K-thesis does not define reality as something that might be but is not.

What might be is the experience of the event, not the event itself. The event goes unperceived even though some nondivine form of awareness could have perceived it. Another way to see this is that, according to the K-thesis, it is an essential property of any reality that it can be perceived. Unless there is a contradiction or a paradox in a thing having the property of being a possible object of awareness, Hartshorne's first argument against the K-thesis must be deemed unsuccessful.

The other two arguments against the K-thesis are employed more often and are much more difficult to answer. Hartshorne argues that since there are limits to nondivine clarity, reality cannot be defined in terms of possible nondivine awareness; " . . . all our knowledge, even of the most obvious events, is approximate at best." (CS 287). There is a strong case for what Hartshorne says. Indeed, it seems that the clarity of any nondivine perception is gained only at the cost of making other things less clear. If I am to adequately hear my parakeet's song, I must attend to his chirps and force the noise from the refrigerator, the heater, and the street into the background of my consciousness. Examples not dealing with the senses are also available. Even in intellectual pursuits, clarity is achieved only at the price of selectivity. It would require a mind of unlimited capacity to process information to be clear about everything. No nondivine awareness could possibly fit this description.

The supporter of the K-thesis might reply: although in any particular experience, some things remain relatively unclear, it is still true that the things that are unclear might have been clear, and this is all the K-thesis requires. The parakeet's song is the focus of the actual experience. But the song might as easily have been in the background with the hum of the refrigerator being the focus of attention.

Hartshorne could agree with the counter-argument but would maintain that, no matter how clear any nondivine experience might be, it is never perfectly clear. Even when focusing on the parakeet's song, there are things that slip by my consciousness, nuances of tone, subtle changes of feeling and a thousand other unnamable shades of meaning: unless, per impossible, I were God, there are an indefinite number of things that escape my awareness. It matters not that I can imagine myself with a better trained ear for birdsong. No matter how well trained the ear, there will be elements that go unnoticed. This is just to say that there are, necessarily, limits to the clarity of any nondivine awareness. We can probably never know what these limits are since such knowledge would itself carry us beyond the limits. Nevertheless, that there are limits to clarity is, I think, incontestable.

The third argument against the K-thesis is that there are things which no nondivine individual could know. This argument has a tendency to be confused with the previous argument. Thus, Hartshorne says,

> . . . does one persuade oneself that there is nothing past we could not know? Every moment each of us has experiences that in their concrete specificity will never be known to anyone else, and eventually we shall not know them either, even in the limited sense in which we ever did know them from memory. (CS 287)

While it is true that we are never completely clear about our own experiences, they are, nevertheless, *our* experiences, and, however inadequately, we are aware of them. This is the problem of clarity again. But are there things that no nondivine individual could know, either clearly or unclearly? Hartshorne asks us to "consider the array of events in galactic space. No animal explorer will ever have more than a vanishingly small fraction of this array in his consciousness." (CS 287). This is most certainly true, and casts a good deal of doubt on the K-thesis. But the defender of the K-thesis may insist that there is absolutely no event, however remote, that some nondivine individual could not know if properly situated. Although we can actually know only a small fraction of the "array of events in galactic space," it may still be true that none of those events are humanly unknowable. I think this position requires a great leap of the imagination, especially in light of the fact that there are probably conditions in the universe under which no human could survive—inside the event horizon of a black hole for example. If the defender of the K-thesis disagrees, there is yet a more damning argument to be given. Consider the example discussed in chapter V, "there are three successive sevens in the decimal determination of π." If this proposition is false, no nondivine individual could know it to be false. Now, the proposition may be true, in which case it can be known to be true by a nondivine individual. But what is important for our purposes is that, for all we know, it is false that the decimal determination of π has three sevens in a row. The example demonstrates that it is perfectly reasonable to believe that some things are humanly (or nondivinely) unknowable. But if this is so, then it is reasonable to believe that the K-thesis is false.

For those who wish to remain atheists, there are only two alternatives at this juncture. They may claim that some things are simply unknowable, or they may say that, although God does not exist, reality is the possible content of divine knowledge (A3). The first alternative divorces the concept of reality from experience which, as we have seen, is problematic. The second alternative is not even coherent. One cannot be an atheist and define reality as what God would know if he existed. For the possible content of ideal knowledge includes knowledge of the ideal knower. Hartshorne makes the same point, "If God does not exist, one thing is true which he could not and would not know if he did exist, namely his own nonexistence." (CS 287). Another problem with A3 (that Hartshorne does not mention) is that, if reality is the possible content of divine knowledge, it follows that it is possible for God to exist. The validity of the ontological argument makes such an admission fatal to the atheist. If God's existence is possible then it is not impossible. And since God's existence is either impossible or necessary, it follows that God exists.[10]

Perhaps the most plausible atheistic position is to modify A2 and say that most real things are knowable, and that those things that are not knowable are, in a sense, within the scope of our knowledge. The unknowable is within the scope of our knowledge in the sense that we have an idea of what kinds of things are unknowable (for example, the complete decimal determination of π). In this respect, the unknowable differs from Kant's noumenal reality. We simply have no concept of what noumenal reality would be like. But we do have a good idea of what it means for there to be (or not to be) three successive sevens in the decimal determination of π. If π does not have three successive sevens, this means that, no matter how far the division is carried out (that is, dividing the circumference of the circle by its diameter), there will never be three sevens in a row. Although it will never be possible to know that there are not three successive sevens in π, we at least know what the proposition entails in humanly experiencable terms.

Although the modified version of A2 is not obviously incoherent or inconsistent, it is still unacceptable. In the first place, it leaves unresolved the problem of the clarity of nondivine experience mentioned above. Second, it is not clear that a theistic assumption has not been smuggled into the description of the unknowable. We are told that, if the proposition about π is false, then no matter how far the division for π is carried out, three successive sevens will never appear. But what nondivine individual (or even race of individuals) would be around long enough to carry out the division? If it is possible to carry division out for an infinite time, as would be required for any transcendental number, it is possible only for God. Apart from the possibility of a divine individual, how can meaning be attached to the idea of carrying out division indefinitely? The atheist might fall back on the distinction between logical and ontological possibility and say that although it is ontologically impossible to divide infinitely, it is logically possible. But this will not do since it is tantamount to admitting that God's existence is logically possible—the concept of a divine experience is thus smuggled in again. If not inconsistent, the position is at least paradoxical.

Whatever other problems it may have, the theistic position does not share the paradoxes of the first three alternatives. Reality is simply the content of divine awareness. We have seen that no amount of nondivine experience can possibly serve to delimit the real. According to Hartshorne—following the suggestion of Royce—this is because of defects internal to nondivine knowledge.

> Our knowledge is non-eminent because of internal characteristics; confusion, inconsistency, doubt, inconstancy of beliefs, and, above all, a lack of concepts adequate to interpret our percepts and of percepts adequate to distinguish between false and true concepts. (CS 288).

It is not that parts of reality are humanly unknowable because of some property that the real possesses. It is because of some defects within our own (or any nondivine) cognitive apparatus, that something of the real always escapes us. To make the mind more perfect is to make its grasp of reality more perfect. Thus, an infallible mind would have an infallible awareness of the real. This allows us to *define* reality as the content of ideal knowledge.

> Instead of saying that eminent knowledge is that which knows everything, we can say, 'everything' is simply the entire content of eminent knowledge, defining the latter without reference to 'reality'. (CS 288).

There is, therefore, no need to presuppose the concept of reality in defining omniscience. The importance of this Roycean insight is that it allows us to contrast nondivine knowledge, not with an anonymous and unknowable stuff, but with the content of an ideal awareness. We can make sense of the idea that the real is the knowable without falling prey to the paradoxes of making nondivine awareness the measure of reality. As Hartshorne says,

> The [theistic] account gives a positive definition of "reality" in terms of something known, namely, the internal characters of knowledge, whereas other views either fail to give a positive definition, or imply that the universe depends upon the human mind.[11]

We mentioned in the opening statement that Hartshorne corrects flaws in traditional statements of Idealism which tend to invalidate the epistemic argument. One of these flaws has already been mentioned, namely, the failure to account for the principle of Objective Independence. The problem is corrected by revising the concept of the ideal knower so that his knowledge has a contingent aspect. A similar move can rescue Idealism from other difficulties. It was long maintained that ideal knowledge must include detailed information about all future events. The paradoxes associated with this position were outlined in chapter III. Admit a contingent side of God and the problems vanish. God's knowledge changes; as future becomes past, things are added to God's knowledge. Since the future is not there to be known (in all its definiteness) until it becomes past, there is no sense in saying that the growth in God's knowledge is a result of divine ignorance. As Hartshorne says,

> Our imperfection in knowledge of the future lies, not in its leaving details unspecified, but in its failure to exhibit clearly how far and in what respects the future is determinate and how far indeterminate.[12]

The ideal knower would be perfectly aware of the extent to which the future is determinate.

Another problem infecting traditional Idealism that is solved by admitting contingency into the divine life is the problem of conceiving God's knowledge as generating its objects. Several problems confront the traditional view. One is that in knowing evil, God creates it. Another is that things seem to become little more than ideas in the mind of God. The combination of these leads to the ingenious but grotesque theodicy of someone like James Ross who maintains that God has no more of an obligation to make his creatures happy than Shakespeare had to make Hamlet happy.[13] We do not deny that these problems have other, more plausible solutions within the framework of classical theism. But another option is simply to abandon the idea that God's knowledge generates its objects. For Hartshorne, it is only because there is something relatively independent of God, that he can know it.

> To say that our "being" is our presence to God is the same as to say that our being is our act of modifying the divine awareness. Ideal knowledge is as truly ideal passivity as it is ideal activity.[14]

This view answers the Kantian objection that we have no concept of what it would be for God to know the world. God's knowledge, like all nondivine knowledge must conform to the object of awareness. The difference between the two forms of knowing is that God's knowledge is unsurpassably more adequate than any nondivine form of awareness. This view parts from the classical theistic doctrine that divine knowledge constitutes its objects. Hartshorne notes that "classical theism made divine properties not only different in kind but opposite rather than unsurpassable. Not supremely sensitive and responsive but wholly insensitive and unresponsive (impassable)."[15]

The passivity in God's cognitive life also answers the objection that God must be a solipsist. Although, in a sense, God knows only himself (since the universe is conceived as God's body), it is also true that his self-knowledge involves knowledge of others. Each nondivine individual leaves an indelible mark in the divine memory. There is a logical gulf between the claim that there is nothing outside God's awareness and the claim that God is a solipsist.

We come finally to the question of whether the epistemic argument proves the existence of God or merely the existence of an ideal knower. As noted in chapter V, an omniscient being would not be anything less than a necessary being. For if it could fail to exist there are things it could fail to know. Must an omniscient being also be all-loving and all-powerful? A plausible case can be made for this even apart from the other elements of the global argument. If, as Hartshorne maintains, knowledge inclusive of the actual concrete feeling of others is some kind of sympathetic participation or love (*NT* 13), then the ideal limit of knowledge would be the ideal of sympathetic participation. God must love his creatures to adequately know them (*RSP* 189 and *CS* 262–263). Furthermore, a being absolute in awareness could not help but be absolute in power. Existence itself is the power to be and if an omniscient being is a necessary being, then it has unlimited power for existence. What more power could there be? This is not to say that God has the power to do anything that is logically possible. It is logically possible that every criminal in the United States will turn himself or herself in to the authorities. But these would be the decisions of criminals, not of God. God has all the power he logically could have. But he is not the only individual with power. I conclude that the epistemic argument, if it proves anything, proves nothing less than the existence of God. Let us turn, now, to the moral argument for God's existence.

VIII
The Moral Argument

Moral arguments for the existence of God come in a variety of forms. The basic pattern of argument is to show that God's existence is implied, presupposed or made probable by moral categories. Kant's version of the argument is the most famous.[1] But others have used the argument in one way or another to support theism.[2] Hartshorne continues this tradition. Given the frequency with which he refers to the argument there is good reason to believe it is one of his favorite proofs for God's existence.[3] The argument is often referred to only in passing. But, aside from *Creative Synthesis* (1970), more or less extensive discussions of the argument are found as early as 1934.[4] The most recent discussions of the moral argument were in 1972 and 1982.[5]

Hartshorne's moral argument is actually a defense of what he calls contributionism, the view that the purpose of human life is to contribute value to the divine life through our creative activity. Traditional concepts of God which imply the complete immutability of the divine cannot countenance such a view. Only a concept of God which allows for a passive side of the divine life could incorporate contributionism. For this reason, Hartshorne's moral argument is unlike other versions. It is, therefore, a standing refutation of the claim that no new theistic proofs are possible.

The Hartshornean moral argument runs as follows. The first three alternatives are found unacceptable either by reason of insoluble paradoxes or contradictions. Only the theistic option can make sense of our moral life.

A1   There is no supreme aim or *summum bonum* whose realization a creature's action can promote.

A2   There is a supreme aim, which is to promote the good life among some (or all) creatures during their natural life spans.

A3   There is a supreme aim, which is to promote the good life among creatures after death or in heaven.

107

T   There is a supreme aim, which is to enrich the divine life (by promoting the good life among creatures). (CS 286–287).

The theistic option includes what is best in the other alternatives, " . . . every legitimate aim which an unbeliever can have, such as promoting human happiness, is included in the aim of serving God."[6] This is a familiar theme of Christian ethics. One cannot love God without loving his creatures. The first Epistle of John (4.21) says, " . . . he who loves God should love his brother also." Love of God is inseparable from love of man. Thus, anyone arguing for any of the three nontheistic alternatives cannot do so on the grounds that theism excludes some value that another option embraces. If theism is mistaken at all, it is because of an overstatement, not an understatement. "The humanistic objectives are entirely embraced in theistic religion."[7]

The moral argument is doomed from the beginning if no good reason can be found to believe that there is a supreme aim, whatever it might be. The view that there is no supreme aim is called ethical relativism. A good example of relativism is in the philosophy of Westermarck. Given the bewildering variety of ethical systems and cultural norms, ethical relativism takes on an air of plausibility. Furthermore, a case can be made that, as Westermarck argues, a belief in relativism can increase tolerance for divergent views.[8]

Hartshorne uses a familiar argument against the relativist's position. "If there is no supreme aim, there is no reasonable idea of comparative values and importance." (CS 289). In order to make sense of comparative value judgments such as "X is better than Y" there must be a standard in terms of which the judgment is made. This argument is, however, incomplete. In his discussion of the moral argument Tennant says,

Our moral experience, evaluation, progress, etc., presuppose norms and ideals; but it is no more obvious that they presuppose an absolute, infinite, or perfect norm than that our growth in stature presupposes the existence, or even the idea, of an infinitely tall giant.[9]

The relativist can agree that comparative value judgments presuppose a standard of value. But he or she is not obliged to agree that the standared is itself nonrelative.

The relativist must retreat into a nonabsolute value standard. This move has problems of its own which G. E. Moore has seen. Hartshorne paraphrases Moore's argument,

> Granting that this or that is preferred or enjoyed by this or that person or group of persons, we can still ask meaningfully, . . . whether or not it is good that it should be enjoyed. (BH 63).

Of any nonabsolute standard of value in terms of which the relativist chooses to measure ethical principles, there is always the further question of whether the standard is itself good. A similar question does not apply to standards of height. Thus, Tennant's analogy between standards of value and quantitative standards (such as those used to measure growth) breaks down. Without the absolute standard, comparative value judgments are rendered completely arbitrary so far as goodness is concerned.

The relativist may insist that Moore's argument applies to the absolute standard itself. Could we not ask of the absolute standard if it is itself good? This question betrays a misunderstanding of the argument. There is nothing beyond the absolute since it is that in terms of which things are measured. Hartshorne agress with Plato that, "the perfect is the measure of itself and of the imperfect." (BH 63). An analogy with a popular criticism of the cosmological argument is instructive. Russell rejected the argument to a first cause on the grounds that one could always ask what caused the first cause.[10] If one of the premises of the first cause argument were that everything has a cause, then Russell's criticism would be valid. But no serious defender of the first cause argument uses such a premise. Rather, the first, or supreme cause is said to make the chain of relative or secondary causes intelligible. Moore's argument should be construed along similar lines. It is not that *every* judgment of value requires, as it were, a standard lying in back of the judgment. Rather, comparative value judgments are made intelligible only on the supposition that there is a standard. And, like the first cause which is its own explanation for being, the absolute standard of value is the measure of itself.

The next view that Hartshorne attacks can be labeled humanism (for lack of a better term). Humanist thinkers wishing to avoid the pitfalls of relativism, affirm that the aim of human life is to promote the good life among some, or all, creatures as far as possible. Since the humanist usually believes there is no afterlife, obligations to fellow creatures are confined to this life. The humanist may adopt one of two views. First, one may believe that one's primary duty is to oneself. In that case, promoting the good life among others is simply a means to one's own satisfaction. I once heard of a wealthy businessman who, though he refused to tithe to any church, made a policy early in life to tithe 10% to himself. It is probably stretching the meaning of the idea of humanism to call this view humanistic. One can only agree with Harthshorne when he says, "If one seeks only one's own good and takes others as mere means to this, one is unethical and indeed more or less inhuman." (CS 289). The humanist may, however, adopt a less egoistic view and insist that one's primary obligation is to increase the general welfare, either among a particular social group, or among humanity in general. Hartshorne claims that the humanistic views share the common problems "death and the multiplicity of benefici-aries." (CS 289). Let us examine each problem in turn.

Hartshorne believes that both individuals and the human race are mortal. Most humanists would agree. The problem is that, after the final extinction of the human race, any values that may have been achieved by the individuals of the race, will become as if they had never been. Russell expressed this idea poignantly,

> . . . all the labors of the ages, all the devotion, all the inspira-
> tion, and all the noonday brightness of human genius, are
> destined to extinction in the vast death of the solar system,
> . . . the whole temple of man's achievement must inevitably
> be buried beneath the debris of a universe in ruins . . . [11]

The outcome of all ethical action—indeed of *all* action—on such a hypothesis, is the same as if no action had been performed. In con-nection with the Buddhist concept that nothing is permanent (pra-tityasamutpada), Hartshorne asks, "If all things are impermanent why does this not render all achievement, including that of becoming en-lightened, completely vain?"[12] Both humanists and nonhumanists agree that some actions are better than others. Presumably this is because good deeds make, or tend to make, the world a better place. When faced with the choice between being kind and being indifferent to a stranger, one should be kind. But if, in the end, the universe swallows the human race leaving no trace of its activities, how has the kind deed made the world a better place?

The humanist can reply to Hartshorne's argument in at least two ways. In the first place, the argument assumes that the consequences of a deed are relevant to its moral worth. Kant explicitly denounced all appeals to consequences as irrelevant to true morality. Thus, what happens 'in the long run' or 'in the end' has nothing to do with ethical decision making. Second, the humanist can claim that, although, in the end, it will not be a good thing that the kind deed was performed, it will nevertheless be true, in the end, that a kind deed was performed. The goodness or value of the deed vanishes with the destruction of mankind, but the truth that the deed *was* good and valuable does not vanish.

Hartshorne rejects both of the humanist's counterarguments. Against Kant it can be argued that between "consequences are never relevant to morality" and "consequences are definitive of moral choice," there is a third position: "consequences are one factor, but not the only factor, in moral choice." It is questionable morality to sacrifice one innocent person for the happiness of many. On the other hand, performing an act with no thought of the possible consequences, is equally objectionable. The command to promote the general welfare cannot serve as the foundation of an ethical system. But surely it must have an important place in any such system. "In ethics, we need to assume that, taking their consequences into account, some modes of action are better than others."[13]

The second humanist argument is more subtle. Even if it is not *good* now, that such and such took place, is it not *true* now, that it occurred? Hartshorne replies that the truth of a proposition about value is the reality of the value asserted (*BH* 14). If it is true that X is good, then the goodness of X is real. To say that it is true *now* that a kind deed was performed is tantamount to saying that the kindness of the deed *is* real. It is not enough to say that the kindness was real, but now is not. For this means that something has become nothing—the value that once was, no longer is. To be sure, it is important to see that it is a past value, not a present value, which is being indicated. But for all its 'pastness', the value is still real. As Hartshorne says, "the past must be capable of containing value." (*BH* 14). Humanists, however, can find no place for past value in their ontology. They might say that the past value is simply 'in the world'. This answer is of little help since the question is how past values can be real; and what is it to be real except to be in the world? Hartshorne's answer to the question of how past values are real is that God infallibly remembers all that occurs. He says that "the only ascertainable value of the past is in its preservation through memory in the present." (*BH* 14).

No finite mind could contain the total reality of the past in memory, since its capacity for memory is, by definition, limited. Something of what Hartshorne means is captured in these lines from Jorge Luis Borges.

> Events far-reaching enough to people all space, whose end is nonetheless tolled when one man dies, may cause us wonder. But something, or an infinite number of things, dies in every death, unless the universe is possessed of a memory . . . [14]

According to Hartshorne, the universe *is* possessed of a memory, the divine memory. Only the hypothesis of a divine remembrance can explain how the past, with all of its values, can be real. There is, of course, the argument that the accuracy of memory is to be measured in terms of reality, not reality in terms of memory. While this is true in the case of finite memories, it is not clear that it applies to the divine memory. Would not reality be synonymous with the content of omniscience? Indeed, this was the point of our previous chapter.

If it is admitted that the death of the human race is a serious problem for a humanist ethic, it is still open to humanists to deny that the race is bound for extinction. This is, perhaps, the most promising line for humanists to take. Hartshorne argued against this position, at one time, as follows,

> At any finite time in the future human power will not be absolute. This means that human security will not be absolute, that there always will be a finite risk of the ending of the human adventure through disease, race suicide, stellar collision, or what not. A finite risk, endured for infinite time, looks like an infinite probability of destruction. (*BH* 65, also *BH* 12).

This argument is valid only if we assume that risk increases with time. But the assumption is questionable. Modern weapons technology has, to be sure, increased the risk of race suicide through global thermonuclear war. But such increases in risk are balanced by other considerations. The risk of the race dying as a result of the plague was once very great. But, because of advances in medical science this particular risk has diminshed. Or again, it is very likely that we will colonize space. This decreases the risk that the entire race could be killed by some sort of stellar collision. Thus, it is not clear that risk increases with time. It is just as plausible to believe that risk remains, more or less constant.[15] It is therefore not beyond the realm of conceivability that the human race will last forever.

Hartshorne seems to have modified his position on the possibility of the extinction of the human race. His latest statements on the issue make the more modest claims that the race cannot be known to be immortal and that the race will, if given enough time, "change beyond any knowable limit."[16] These claims, I think, are undeniable. Hartshorne points out that the lack of knowledge of what the future holds is a problem for the humanist,

> Since we cannot possibly have any definite knowledge, or even imagining, of such an infinity of human survival, our basic ethical notion of ultimate consequences seems to vanish into total indefiniteness.[17]

Theists have a distinct advantage over humanists insofar as the ultimate consequences of our deeds are forever stored in the mind of God. For humanists, it must be admitted that, since the collective memory of humankind is so fragmentary, even the greatest of deeds of the greatest of men and women, will someday be forgotten. We have turned full circle to the problem of past values.

Death is not the only difficulty facing humanists. There is also what Hartshorne calls the problem of the multiplicity of beneficiaries. Implicit in the injunction to promote the general welfare is the notion that, all things being equal, the more individuals that are happy, the better. A corollary of this is that it is worse for two to suffer than for one to suffer. Apart from the existence of a being "to whom all hearts are open," it is not clear how to make sense of these ideas. Hartshorne says,

> Good is good *for* someone. How is the welfare of A plus the welfare of B a greater good than that of either alone? The sum of happiness, for whom is this happiness? (CS 289).

C. S. Lewis clearly expressed the opposite view. Although he was a theist, Lewis did not believe there is any such thing as the 'sum of suffering' or the 'sum of happiness'.

> Suppose that I have a toothache of intensity x: and suppose that you, who are seated beside me, also begin to have a toothache of intensity x. You may, if you choose, say that the total amount of pain in the room is 2x. [Should Lewis have

said "x + x" instead?] But you must remember that no one is
suffering 2x: search all time and space and you will not find
that composite pain in anyone's consciousness. There is no
such thing as a sum of suffering. When we have reached the
maximum that a single person can suffer, we have, no doubt,
reached something very horrible, but we have reached all
the suffering there ever can be in the universe. The addition
of a million fellow-sufferers adds no more pain.[18]

Despite Flew's implications to the contrary, Lewis does not mean to
deny that, all else being equal, more suffering is worse.[19] Lewis's point
is that the atheist gains an unfair emotive advantage in debates on
the problem of evil by speaking in vague terms about the "unimagin-
able sum of human misery." The Hartshornean problem, however,
remains: if there is no such thing as a sum of suffering how is it worse
when two are in pain than when one is in pain? There is no one for
whom it is worse.

Hartshorne believes that the problem arises even if we consider only
one person, "we feel that it is more important that a life should be
steadily happy than that there should be a moment or two of happiness
during its course." (CS 289). In the case of only one individual, however, it can be argued that it is better or worse for the person involved
that more happiness is enjoyed.[20] But a similar move cannot be made
when more than one person's happiness is in question. Hartshorne's
answer to the problem is that it is worse, for God, when there is more
suffering than there should have been. If the values of the world are
incorporated into the divine consciousness, then clear meaning can
be given to the idea that more suffering is worse and that more happiness is better.

Humanists might reply as follows: the suffering of A and B is more
suffering than that of A alone, not in the sense that someone suffers
the suffering of A and B, but only in the sense that the number two
is greater than the number one. Since it is true that "2 > 1" it follows
that two instances of suffering are greater than one instance of suffering. This argument hinges on an ambiguity in the concept of "being
greater than." Humanists and theists can agree that the suffering of
two persons is *numerically* greater than the suffering of only one. But
only the neoclassical theist can make sense of the belief that the suffering of A and B is worse than, or a greater evil than the suffering
of A alone. Another way to put the question is to ask how a numerical
difference could make a qualitative or moral difference.

Another humanist reply is that since it is one's duty to promote the general welfare, the general welfare must be good. Asking why the general welfare is good is like asking why one should be moral. But the reason for being moral lies within the sphere of morality itself—one should be moral because it is the right thing to do. This reply masks a subtle confusion. It is true that morality justifies itself, but it is not obvious that asking for an explanation of why the general welfare is good is equivalent to asking why one should be moral. If the general welfare is a good, then it is true that one has an obligation to promote the good. The problem is that, on humanist principles, there seems to be no account of why the general welfare is a good. But if it is not a good, then whence comes the duty to promote it? An act is not good because there is a duty to perform it, there is a duty to perform it because it is good.

An interesting consequence of the problem of multiple beneficiaries is that it shows that one form of the problem of evil is self-defeating. As noted in chapter VI, Madden and Hare argue that the existence of God is made improbable given the enormous amount of suffering in the world. If Hartshorne's argument is correct, then the only possible way to make sense of the idea of an enormous amount of suffering is on the theistic hypothesis. If one denies the existence of God, then one must accept Lewis's argument that there is no such thing as a sum of suffering. But with no sum of suffering, the major premise of the Madden and Hare argument collapses.

The final alternative in the moral argument, before the theistic option, also suffers from the problem of multiple beneficiaries. The last option says that the supreme aim is to promote the good life among creatures after death or in heaven. Supposing that the soul survives the death of the body, this by itself could not explain why the happiness of two disembodied spirits is better than the happiness of one. There are other problems as well. One problem is, perhaps, more psychological than philosophical. Few atheists can bring themselves to believe in an afterlife. Thus, most atheists would opt for A2 over A3. Hartshorne's only serious opponents, as far as A3 is concerned, are other theists, not atheists.

Rather than rehearse the now familiar arguments against classical theism covered in our second chapter, let us only be reminded that the view that creatures can in no way add to the value in God forces one to believe that the supreme aim in life is to promote the good life among creatures, whether during their natural lives or after death. In what way this aim could also be considered a service or a benefit to

God has never been made clear by classical theists. God, classically conceived, is self-sufficient and unchanging. Since the total content of value in the divine life is forever fixed, God is the only individual who adds value to the lives of others. Others, in no way, add to the value in God. We can do nothing for God, but he does everything for us. Kant brings this out most clearly. By providing an afterlife in which the injustices of earthly existence are set straight, God does for his creatures what they could not do for themselves.

Apart from the doctrine of an immutable deity, neoclassical theism can accept much of the Kantian picture. Lewis Ford and Marjorie Suchocki have shown how Whitehead's metaphysics, which is not so different from Hartshorne's views, can account for a kind of subjective immortality.[21] Hartshorne rejects the idea of personal immortality on the grounds that a nondivine individual could undergo only a finite number of changes before becoming a different person (*LP* 261).[22] One could accept this argument but still believe in a limited immortality in which many of the injustices of earthly existence are compensated in a life to come. There may be a point at which one's personal experiences come to an end, but it may not be what we call natural death.[23]

Hartshorne clearly rejects this view. Not even God can eliminate risk of failure; and thus, an afterlife could not solve the problem of injustice. I do not think this argument is conclusive. May not God isolate some of those who died prematurely or suffered unjustly and allow them to enjoy a little more happiness without thereby eliminating the risks that were involved in bringing about the injustices? It would remain eternally true that risks had been taken and that tragedy occurred. God's redeeming action might be interpreted simply as a more complete revelation of his own love before the final (not the earthly) death of the individual. This view has the advantage of permitting more good to come to those who have suffered unjustly without denying that a greater amount of good could have been achieved had the suffering never occurred. Such a view of the afterlife differs from traditional views in that the individual is not born into another social world. The individual is related only to God after death, who reveals himself in more fullness to the survivor. But this view is like the traditional view in that a final chapter is, so to speak, added to the individual's life. The individual's life then resembles more a completed work than a half written text.[24] Thus, I do not find the notion of a limited immortality with a limited compensation for injustices obviously incompatible with Hartshorne's metaphysics. Without denying the reality of creaturely freedom, this is all any theist could reasonably ask. Since traditional theism can provide no more than neoclassical theism, the latter is to be preferred, insofar as it allows for a meaningful concept of service to God.

If it is a good thing to contribute to the divine life, then the divine life must be good. Thus, Hartshorne's moral argument, combined with the other arguments in his cumulative case, gives reason to believe in a good, all-powerful, all-knowing, and necessary being. There are, to be sure, problems in construing God's goodness as a form of moral goodness. As Ninian Smart argues, an agent who infallibly chooses the good and faces no temptation for evil is not clearly a moral agent.[25] Nevertheless, it is not a misuse of the concept of goodness to call such an agent good. God is a person's ultimate good in the sense of being the most adequate fulfillment of his or her desires. As Hartshorne says, "It is not my death, but God's that would make my life a mere absurdity."[26] The value of a human life is, then, its contribution to the divine life. Hartshorne expresses the central idea of the moral argument.

> Unchangeably right and adequate is his manner of changing in and with all things, and unchangeably immortal are all changes, once they have occurred, in the never darkened expanse of his memory, the treasure house of all fact and attained value. (MVG 298).

This brings us to the frontiers of the aesthetic argument for God's existence, wherein we might catch a glimpse of the grandeur of God's eternal vision.

IX

The Aesthetic Argument

The aesthetic argument is the last of the theistic proofs in Hartshorne's cumulative case. Although Hartshorne told me that he views the aesthetic argument as his most original contribution to the global argument, it is the argument least often mentioned in his work. This is not to say that Hartshorne has been silent on the relation between God and beauty. Entire chapters are devoted to the topic in early works.[1] But it is not until A *Natural Theology for Our Time* (1967) and *Creative Synthesis* (1970) that the concept of beauty is used as a way to prove God's existence. In one respect, this is surprising. For Hartshorne has always maintained an active interest in aesthetics. Aesthetic principles play a central role in both *The Philosophy and Psychology of Sensation* and *Born to Sing* (these being the least metaphysical of Hartshorne's books).[2] On the other hand, the absence of the aesthetic argument in most of Hartshorne's work is not so surprising. For in many ways, the aesthetic proof is simply a variation of themes running through the other proofs, especially the epistemic. With only minor variations, the arguments supporting the premises of the epistemic argument also support the premises of the aesthetic argument. There is, however, enough novelty in the aesthetic proof to warrant separating it from the other arguments. Yet another facet of the problem of divine reality is revealed in this argument from beauty.

The argument runs as follows:

A1　There is no beauty of the world as a (*de facto*) whole.

A2　There is a beauty of the world as a whole, but no one enjoys it.

A3　There is a beauty of the world as a whole, but only non-divine beings enjoy it.

T　　There is a beauty of the world as a whole and God alone adequately enjoys it. (CS 287).

It is significant that Hartshorne speaks of the world as a *de facto* whole. Since he adopts the process view of time, according to which only the past is fully determinate, Hartshorne denies that the world is a completed fact. The world is constantly changing. At any moment, "the world" refers to a different totality. Yesterday's world did not include tomorrow's experiences, except as possibilities. "The creative view of process . . . does not allow the concept of 'all events' as a final totality." (*LP* 98). Thus, if there is a beauty of the world it is dynamic, more akin to the beauty of a dance or a drama than a painting or a sculpture (I am reminded of the Hindu view of creation as the dance of Siva).

The world, as a whole, may lack beauty for two reasons, (1) because the concept of beauty lacks objective reference, or (2) because the universe is, as a matter of fact, not beautiful; that is, either it lacks something that would make it beautiful or possesses some property positively incompatible with beauty. In his brief treatment of AI, Hartshorne deals only with the second point. But many things he says elsewhere make clear how he would respond to the first point. Let us discuss each question in turn.

The position sometimes called aesthetic subjectivism is the view that qualities such as beauty have no objective foundation. It is not that objects have some property called beauty independent of our perception; rather, it is our perception that the object is beautiful which accounts for the object's beauty. "Beauty is in the eye of the beholder" is a popular expression of subjectivism (perhaps more accurately, "Beauty is *merely* in the eye of the beholder"). The clearest example of aesthetic subjectivism is in the philosophy of logical positivism where questions of morality and aesthetics are reduced to matters of personal or societal taste or emotion.[3] Subtler versions of subjectivism have been developed, but all of them share the contention that beauty is something we put in the world, not something we discover there.[4] If subjectivism is true then there could not be an objective beauty of the world as a whole.

Hartshorne's earliest statements on the issue reveal a clear rejection of subjectivism. "Aesthetic experience is not a mere subjective reaction but implies worth in the object . . . " (*OD* 233). Later he would argue against what he called "the annex view of value"—namely, that value is "annexed" onto bare sensations.[5] For Hartshorne, aesthetic subjectivism is a mistake since aesthetic value is essential to all experience. "Absolute aesthetic failure simply means no experience at all." (CS 304). If experience is real, then so is value. Indeed, with each new experience is the production of new value. But then it is misleading and false to call value *merely* subjective. While it is true that the value is in the subject, the subject in turn becomes an object for other subjects. Thus, value is an objective quality. This is manifestly true when the objects in quesiton are other human individuals. The love that I feel for my mother is felt by her as an objective fact. There is a similar feeling of the objectivity of value even in our experience of so called 'inanimate' nature. It is no accident that thunder is felt as threatening or that sunshine is felt as gay. Of course, we can condition ourselves to ignore or alter our feelings towards things. But this is not good evidence for subjectivism. For the alteration in feeling itself presupposes an element of stubborn fact. There is a kind of heroism in overcoming a fear of thunder, and an element of pathetic tragedy in becoming blinded to the gaiety of sunshine.

The fact of disagreement on aesthetic matters is sometimes taken as an argument against the objectivity of aesthetic value.[6] But the argument is particularly weak. Since when did disagreement imply that questions of truth are not at stake? Furthermore, disagreements are balanced by general uniformities of opinion. As Hartshorne says,

> [the value of] a flaming sunset, a rose with its color and odor, or the blue sky, are obvious facts. A man who questioned many of these judgments in genuine honesty would hardly be thought sane—if his sense organs were thought to be healthy. (*OD* 234)

The same points apply to disagreements between cultures. Indeed, if there were not some common ground for aesthetic taste, how could one make sense of the influence of one culture upon another? A sharing of values implies a common ground, just as exchange of currency implies a global standard. Thus, the disagreements that exist between cultures are compatible with aesthetic objectivism. On the other hand, the tremendous level of shared opinion remains an embarrassment to aesthetic subjectivism.

If it is not because beauty is merely subjective that the world as a whole is not beautiful, perhaps it is because the world lacks something that would make it beautiful, or possesses a quality incompatible with beauty. That the world has the necessary conditions for being beautiful seems clear enough. If anything is agreed on in philosophy, it is that beauty is somehow a proper balance between unity and variety. Hartshorne characterizes this as "coherent diversity."[7] The repetition of a musical chord is monotonous whereas the random sound of notes is chaotic. Neither is beautiful. But combine the notes and chords into a melody and something beautiful can emerge. The world has the necessary components of unity and variety.

> Is the universe as a whole beautiful? Certainly it contains
> more contrasts than anything else, for all contrasts fall within
> it. And it does have unity. Physics discovers the same kinds
> of matter, the same laws, even in the most distant heavenly
> bodies . . . (MVG 213).

In light of these considerations we can at least say that the world has aesthetic value. But it does not follow from a thing having aesthetic value that it is beautiful. A simple melody has aesthetic value, but it need not be beautiful. Hartshorne says "Beauty in the emphatic sense is a *balance* of unity and variety." (CS 304).[8] Does the universe have a proper balance of unity and diversity?

The many instances of suffering may be taken as evidence against the beauty of the world. Does not the enormous amount of suffering imply an insufficient unity in the universe? Several points need to be made in reference to suffering. First, since the beauty of the world as a whole is the point at issue, all of the joy, ecstasy, gaiety and happiness in the universe count as heavily as all of the suffering, pain and misery. It is as true that the suffering of a starving child counts against the world's beauty as that the saintliness of a Mother Theresa counts for it. If theists sometimes seem too callous toward suffering, atheists sometimes seem too insensitive to the beauty in the world. Even taking a simplistic approach to the problem by weighing the number of evil things against the number of good things, it is by no means obvious that the evil outbalances the good. As anyone who takes the trouble to look will see, there is a great deal of good about the world.

The second point about suffering is that, in itself, it is not incompatible with beauty. The beautiful can be tragic as well as sublime. Victor Hugo's Quasimodo is a tragic figure of great beauty. Even the atheistic existentialists do not appear to deny that there is a beauty in the defiance of an absurd universe.

The final point about suffering concerns the moral argument. If the moral argument is sound, then the notion of the "sum of suffering" is intelligible only on theistic grounds. To deny the world's beauty on the basis that it contains a great deal of suffering implies a theistic metaphysic. The atheist would be caught in the dilemma: either suffering does not count against the world's beauty or it does. In case of the latter, God exists. In light of these considerations, an appeal to suffering as evidence against the world's beauty is, at best, problematic and, at worst, a paradox.

Is the world as a whole beautiful? Hartshorne argues that if it were not beautiful

> the world would be either chaos or a mere monotony. Neither is possible, the first for the same reason as holds against [the claim that there is no cosmic order], the second for the reason that order implies a contrasting element of disorder . . . (CS 289-290).

We have already seen that between the extremes of chaos (or sheer diversity) and monotony (sheer unity) there are a variety of aesthetic values, not all of which are beautiful. Beauty is a proper balance between unity and diversity. As it stands, Hartshorne's argument proves only that the world has aesthetic value, not that it is beautiful. How might the argument be supplemented?

If the aesthetic argument is to be *a priori*, then it must not simply be a contingent fact that the world as a whole is beautiful, it must be a necessary truth. This fact provides the clue to how Hartshorne's argument against A1 must be supplemented. We have already seen that it is a necessary truth that something exists (cosmological argument) and that there is a cosmic order (design argument). It should also be evident by now that it is necessarily true that the world has aesthetic value. For if reality is defined in terms of experience and experience is essentially aesthetic then, if the world is real, it has aesthetic value. Concerning necesssary truths Hartshorne says,

> With metaphysical or *a priori* and necessary statements, it is impossible that these statements could be true and yet also have negative value in any reasonable sense. Contingent facts can be regrettable, but this may not be said of necessary truths. For to say "regrettable" is to say that it would have been better had they not obtained, and this makes sense only if the truths are contingent.[9]

If this is true then the aesthetic value of the world cannot be regrettable; it cannot be merely silly, ugly, ridiculous, commonplace or even pretty since these can always be regrettable. The world's value must

consist in an ideal balance between unity and diversity . . . the aesthetic value of the world must be beauty.

A necessary truth can only be regrettable as long as one remains
blind to its necessity. There is still a question, however, how the
nonregrettableness of necessary truths implies their beauty. C. S. Lewis
seems to have denied this implication.

> When once one has dropped the absurd notion that reality is
> an arbitrary alternative to "nothing," one gives up being a
> pessimist (or even an optimist). There is no sense in blaming
> or praising the Whole, nor, indeed, in saying anything about
> it.[10]

Lewis's view is that the necessary aspect of things is value-neutral. It
can be neither cause for remorse nor cause for rejoicing . . . it simply
is.

Hartshorne denies that indifference is a possible response to the
necessary. To be indifferent to something is to fail to find any good
in it. But the minute we think about something we are not totally
indifferent to it, we find something that catches our interest even if
but for a moment. Thus, Hartshorne claims that the necessary cannot
be viewed,

> with mere indifference, for the act of taking note of a thing
> must, like every act, be motivated by some good. The utterly
> indifferent is what we fail to note at all; and when we do
> note it, absolute indifference has been replaced by some valua-
> tion, positive, negative or both.[11]

If, as we have argued, a negative attitude is not appropriate toward
the necessary, and if indifference is not possible, then only a positive
evaluation of the necessary is appropriate. We say "appropriate" ad-
visedly. For there have been those who, if they have not been indifferent to the necessary, have adopted a negative attitude towards it—
Schopenhauer being the best example. But if Hartshorne's argument
is sound, then this is confused thinking. It is possible to be repulsed,
or feel indifference for the necessary only so long as one does not
recognize it for what it is. The only appropriate evaluation of the
necessary is positive. Total indifference is impossible. And if, as already
argued, only the beautiful can be nonregrettable, then the necessary
must be beautiful.

If the necessary aspect of things is beautiful, does it follow that the world as a *de facto* whole is beautiful? According to Hartshorne's metaphysics, the world that actually exists—that is, the current "cosmic epoch"—is not necessary. All that is necessary is that some world or other exists. One must ask whether the beauty of the necessary aspect of the world allows us to infer the beauty of the world as it actually exists. A parallel with the ontological argument is instructive in answering this question.

A common criticism of the ontological argument is that an abstract property such as perfection is on a different logical level than an actually existing individual. One cannot infer from a universal that the universal has an instance, or is exemplified in some concrete particular. Hartshorne's answer to this problem is to claim that the ontological argument can only prove that perfection is *somehow* exemplified, not that it is exemplified in this or that particular way. With ordinary individuals there is a double element of contingency. Whether I exist now as hearing the chimes on the porch or as listening to the parakeet's chirps is a contingent matter. But it is also contingent that I exist. In the case of God, Hartshrone claims, only the former element of contingency applies. It is not contingent that perfection is somehow exemplified. But the particular way in which it happens to be exemplified is contingent. The point is that there are a variety of ways or states in which God can exist. One of God's possible states is knowing me hearing the chimes. Another is knowing me listening to the parakeet. Yet another is knowing that I do not exist. There is nothing necessary about any of these states.

A similar distinction is applicable to the beauty of the world. It is necessarily true that the world is beautiful. But there are a variety of ways in which beauty can be exemplified. Representing possible world states (or cosmic epochs) as B_1, B_2, B_3, . . . B^n we can say that all of them are beautiful. Furthermore, since it is necessary that something exists, one or another of B_1 . . . B^n will be exemplified at any given time. Thus, there will always be a beauty of the world as a *de facto* whole. Since our own world is among the class of B_1, . . . B^n it follows that the actual world, as a whole, is beautiful.

Having established that the world as a *de facto* whole is beautiful, it is a short step to God's existence. Aside from the arguments against A2 and A3 that Hartshorne mentions, there are other considerations. The same arguments that tell against A1 and A2 of the epistemic argument (chapter VII), refute A2 and A3 of the aesthetic argument.

A1 of the epistemic argument says that reality in no way depends upon knowledge. A2 of the aesthetic argument says that there is a beauty of the world but no one enjoys it. If, as we have argued, beauty is an objective quality, then to say that there is a beauty that no one enjoys is to say there is a reality that is not known or experienced. This can mean one of two things, either (1) the world's beauty could be known but is not, as a matter of contingent fact, known, or (2) the world's beauty could not, in principle, be known. (2) is vulnerable to the objection that the only meaning that can be given to the concept of reality is agreement between concepts and percepts. There could be no unexperiencible reality. (1) is subject to the objection that the only possible being who could adequately appreciate the world's beauty is God. Thus, to say the world's beauty could be known is to say that it could be known by God. This is to admit that God's existence is possible. And, by Anselm's principle, the possibility of God's existence implies that God exists.

There is also an obvious parallel between A2 of the epistemic argument and A3 of the aesthetic argument. Both involve the claim that reality is measured by human or non-divine experience. But just as there is more to reality than is humanly knowable, so the world has more beauty than any human (or group of humans) could enjoy. Hartshorne says,

> Beauty as a value is actualized only in experience. However, the concrete beauty of the cosmos . . . could not be adequately appreciated by our fragmentary kind of perception and thought. There can then be an all-inclusive beauty only if there be an all-inclusive appreciation of beauty . . . (NT 15).

The world's treasures are inexhaustible. The process of scientific discovery testifies to this fact. Once it was felt that it was only a matter of time before the methods of science would uncover the whole truth about the world. The actual process of scientific discovery has given the lie to such cognitive megalomania. No sooner is one puzzle solved than ten others seem to take its place. If in some respects the world is like a jigsaw puzzle which scientists carefully piece together, in other respects, it is more like Hydra, the creature of Greek mythology who grew two heads for every one that was severed. With every scientific discovery, something of the beauty of the world is found—and (what is important for our purposes), we catch a glimpse of its limitless riches.

The arguments Hartshorne offers against A2 and A3 (of the aesthetic argument) are also persuasive. In connection with A2—that the beauty of the world is not enjoyed—Hartshorne argues that to have the idea of the beauty of the world is already to enjoy something of its beauty. "There is no experience and no thought absolutely without aesthetic fulfillment." (CS 290). This is not to say that the mere thought of the world's beauty is enough to evoke an adequate appreciation of that beauty. But the thought is not about nothing. If a thought is an experience and if experience always involves some aesthetic value then the thought that the world is beautiful is not without an aesthetic value of its own—however slight that may be.

Against the view that only nondivine beings enjoy the beauty of the world (A3), Hartshorne argues,

> Our enjoyment . . . is utterly disproportionate to the beauty in question. This disproportion would be an absolutely basic flaw in reality, such as never could be eliminated. It must always have obtained, and it could not be merely contingent, but must rather be an eternally necessary yet ugly aspect of things. Always God ought to have existed to enjoy his creation, and always he failed to exist. (CS 290).

One might argue that, although it is a flaw in reality that the world's beauty is enjoyed only by nondivine individuals, the flaw is epistemological, not aesthetic. In other words, if God does not exist to enjoy the beauty of the world, it is simply a fact, not perforce an ugly fact. This argument is mistaken. Ordinarily we consider it a good thing if something beautiful is appreciated; and we consider it regrettable if beauty goes unappreciated. Thus, the disproportion between enjoyment and beauty which would obtain if God did not exist would not be a merely neutral fact—it would be an eternally regrettable flaw in the nature of things. We have already seen that the necessary aspect of things must be beautiful. An eternal, and therefore necessary, flaw in reality is, thus, a contradiction in terms.

An aspect of the nature of God highlighted by the aesthetic argument is the depth and sensitivity involved in omniscience. A being capable of an adequate appreciation of the world's beauty would have to be omniscient since no part of reality could escape its gaze. But the being would also have to possess a level of sensitivity to events far beyond our imagination to conceive. We know that nondivine appreciation of beauty requires a degree of attentiveness that surpasses ordinary practical modes of cognition. To appreciate a painting as more than a thing that covers a wall, it is necessary to allow one's consciousness to focus specifically on the painting, to see the various shades of colors, the contrasts, the geometrical patterns, the hidden meanings. The painting becomes more than pigments on canvas—it is an aesthetic object. If we now take the world as a whole as God's aesthetic object, and magnify what in us is appreciation of beauty, we can understand something of the complexity and subtlety of the divine awareness. Furthermore, if in knowing beauty we contain part of the beautiful within ourselves, then God, who alone adequately beholds the beauty of the world, must be the supremely beautiful object for our own awareness. The aesthetic argument, therefore, can augment not only our understanding of omniscience but it can deepen our concept of the divine goodness.

This concludes our study of the aesthetic proof. We have also reached the last of the elements of the global argument. We have still to tie together the loose ends that remain. This is a topic for our concluding chapter.

X

The Unity of God
and The Balance of Evidence

The global argument is an *a priori* cumulative case for God's existence. The discussion thus far, however, has focused primarily on individual proofs without much attention to the cumulative nature of the arguments. Furthermore, the discussion has largely been supportive of Hartshorne's position. But, as Hartshorne acknowledges, there are problems. Some of these problems have been noted during the course of our discussion. But other problems are broader, touching on issues that go beyond any of the arguments taken individually. The purpose of this chapter, therefore, is twofold. First, I wish to tie together the loose ends of the previous chapters so as to gain a perspective on the global argument as a whole. Second, I will indicate what, to my mind, is the weakest point in Hartshorne's position.

I have already said some things about the interconnections among the various arguments. Let me reiterate and expand on these comments. Perhaps the most important—at any rate, most obvious—point is that all of the arguments depend on the ontological argument for their soundness. As we have seen, Hartshorne believes that the importance of the ontological argument is that it demonstrates that God's existence is either logically necessary or logically impossible. A contingently existing God is a contradiction since perfection of existence implies necessity of existence. Thus, if any of the other arguments only attempted to prove the existence of a contingently existing being, the argument(s) could not be successful. No sound argument can have a false conclusion. If God cannot exist contingently, then no argument purporting to prove the existence of such a God could be sound. This is the sense in which all theistic arguments stand or fall with the success of the ontological proof.

The major weakness Hartshorne sees in the ontological argument is the assumption that it is possible for a logically necessary being to exist. This is the point at which the other proofs can buttress the ontological argument. The cosmological argument is most important in this connection since it demonstrates the inconceivability of absolute nonbeing. Since nonbeing is inconceivable and since no individual or group of individuals existing contingently can account for the necessity of existence, there must be at least one individual who exists necessarily. Thus, if there are contingent beings it is possible that there is a necessary being.

The weakness of the cosmological argument is that it does not specify what attributes a necessary being must have. In our discussion of the cosmological proof the problem of Ahriman, the evil deity, was raised. The moral argument is especially helpful in seeing the absurdity concealed in the notion that God is evil. If the moral argument is sound, then, any conceivable nondivine individual would require a greater reality to which its life could contribute. An evil God could not, in principle, be the ground of meaning in human life. Thus, if God exists, he is good.

By clarifying the concept of omnipotence the design argument is also relevant to the question of God's goodness. Since evil is a nearly inevitable result of creaturely freedom, the notion that God orders the world does not entail that he could prevent every instance of suffering. Any conceivable world would contain a certain amount of disorder and evil. Thus, the existence of suffering in the world is no reflection on God's goodness. Furthermore, it is not clear why an evil deity would be required to explain cosmic order. If, as Hartshorne argues, God includes the world in his being, much as the mind includes the body, then God could accomplish the goal of creating suffering in the world only by harming himself. God could not be a sadist without also being a masochist.

The epistemic and aesthetic arguments also contribute to an understanding of the necessary being of the cosmological argument. The epistemic argument shows that the necessary being is omniscient. Reality cannot be simply unknowable. Since all nondivine knowledge is imperfect, there must be one whose knowledge adequately conforms to the real. Such a being is, by definition, omniscient. The aesthetic argument serves to sharpen the concept of a necessary being even further by demonstrating that the necessary aspect of things must be beautiful.

A deficiency of the global argument is that it does not rule out the possibility that there is more than one necessary being. To some extent, the design argument addresses the question of polytheism. There could not, in principle, be more than one cosmic ordering power.

Thus, there is only one omnipotent being. The question, however, is whether the omnipotent being is the only necessary being. The design argument does not adequately deal with this question.

Hartshorne is not without an answer to the problem of polytheism. According to Hartshorne, "God is the *one individual conceivable a priori.*" (*DR* 31). Ordinary or nondivine individuals are not individuated by concepts alone. As Hartshorne says, "No nondivine individual whatever can be exhausted in a concept or definition." (*NT* 130).[1] Hartshorne's claim can be proven in two ways. First, the concepts that apply to any given individual might have applied to some other individual. Thus, the cluster of concepts that, in the actual world, refer to Socrates—being the teacher of Plato, snubnosed, etc.—could, in some other conceivable state of affairs have referred to someone else. This is not to say that Socrates might not have been Socrates; rather, it is to say that the properties which Socrates actually possessed might have been possessed by someone else. A second proof of Hartshorne's contention is that any nondivine individual might have had properties other than what he actually has. Socrates could have been born without a snubnose, he could have failed to meet Plato, and so forth. Thus, no nondivine individual can be individuated by concepts alone.[2]

God is the one exception to the otherwise applicable rule that individuality is not specifiable *a priori*. The reason that God must be an exception to the rule is that he is the only individual with strictly universal functions. He is the one who, as *all*-powerful, *all*-knowing, and *all*-loving, orders, knows, and loves the world. He is, in Hartshorne's words, *all*-inclusive. Nothing can exist outside the being of God. Hartshorne defines inclusion as follows: X includes Y if X and Y together are no more than X alone, that is, X includes Y if $(X + Y) = X$.[3] From this definition, it is easy to prove that there could be no more than one God. Let X and Y be two all-inclusive beings. It follows that X and Y must include each other. Thus, $(X + Y) = X$ and $(X + Y) = Y$; ergo, $X = Y$. The two all-inclusive beings are really the same thing. God, as the all-inclusive being, is unique. There could not be more than one God.

Hartshorne's argument might be questioned on the grounds that it does not prove that there could not be more than one necessary being. All that is proved is that the all-inclusive reality must be unique. This counter-argument misses the point. Hartshorne rightly identifies God with the all-inclusive reality. If there could be only one all-inclusive reality then there could be only one God. It is no objection to say that there might be beings, besides God, that exist necessarily. The point is that these beings would not be all-inclusive and thus would not be God. Therefore, the existence of many necessary beings does not pose a threat to monotheism.

Although the existence of a multiplicity of necessary beings does not provide a legitimate objection to monotheism, there are arguments which prove that the existence of more than one necessary being is an absurd notion. Duns Scotus has shown most clearly the problem of thinking there could be more than one necessary being.[4] To admit that more than one necessary being exists is to admit that an infinite number of necessary beings exist. Any concept admits of an infinite number of possible instantiations. No matter how many men exist, for example, there could always be more men. The concept of man in no way limits the number of men that could exist. Similarly, if there could be more than one nondivine necessary being, then there is no limit to the number that could exist. The problem is that, in the case of a necessary being, its mere possibility is enough to ensure its actual existence. The ontological argument shows that the concept of a nonexistent necessary being whose existence is logically possible is incoherent. Thus, if there could be an infinite number of necessary beings, these beings must exist. Democritus might have viewed this conclusion as a welcome addition to his atomism. The concept, however, of an infinite number of actually existing nondivine necessary beings is not without its problems. We have already seen, in chapter V, that the concept of the actual infinite, if not contradictory, is paradoxical. Thus, when faced with the choice between one necessary being and an infinite number of necessary beings, one should opt for the former since it involves the least paradox.

Prima facie, there is a tension between our rejection of the actual infinite in the above argument and our acceptance of the actual infinite in chapter V. In truth there is no problem in this strategy. The differences between the two cases are important. The argument of chapter V has to do with the concept of an actually infinite series of events in time. The argument against the existence of an infinity of necessary beings has to do with the simultaneous existence of an actual infinite. It may be the case, as Hartshorne suggests, that problems attending the concept of an infinite temporal series are less severe than problems in the concept of an infinite number of beings existing simultaneously (CS 126).

The most important difference between the arguments of chapter V and the argument against an infinity of necessary beings lies in the use of the principle of least paradox. In chapter V we were faced with two equally paradoxical positions: either there was a first moment of time or there was not. Neither position is free of paradoxical and counter-intuitive consequences. Given this stalemate, the problem had to be settled, at least for the present, by other considerations. Thus, we argued that, if God knows himself, he could never have been without some world or other. The problem of the existence of an infinite number of necessary beings is paradoxical. But the alternative under consideration—that there is only one necessary being— is not obviously paradoxical. Unlike the alternatives of chapter V, both of which involve paradoxes, the alternative to an infinity of necessary beings is unproblematic. The principle of least paradox dictates that the least paradoxical position be accepted. It is more reasonable to believe that there could be only one necessary being. Thus, there is no problem of our acceptance of the actual infinite in chapter V and our rejection of the actual infinite in the present context.

It should be noted that the existence of one necessary being is not the only alternative to the existence of an infinite number of necessary beings. One may choose to believe there are no necessary beings. This simply entails the denial of theism. The last six chapters have been a concerted attempt to show that that denial is not reasonable.

The various components of the global argument tend to support one another. With the arguments against polytheism, Hartshorne's cumulative case takes on additional force. There are, however, soft spots in Hartshorne's chain of reasoning that should be noted. The soft spots are called 'soft' not because I believe Hartshorne's edifice is likely to crumble in these areas but because, in the present work, space did not permit the detailed defense that some of Hartshorne's doctrines require. Let me indicate some of these soft areas.

One of the central pillars of the ontological argument is the theory of temporal possibility. According to this theory, modal distinctions are finally to be understood as temporal distinctions. That is possible which could have arisen in the past or will be capable of arising in the future. It is to Hartshorne's credit to have seen so clearly that, without the theory of temporal possibility, the ontological argument is a failure. If God's existence is logically possible without being really possible, then the inference from "possibly God exists" to "necessarily God exists" is invalid. This is the point of Plantinga's and Hick's criticism of the ontological argument discussed in chapter IV. Thus, those who find the theory of temporal possibililty unacceptable are unlikely to value the ontological argument very highly.

Several reasons can be adduced for denying the theory of temporal possibility. The most obvious argument, however, is that some disciplines seem, to some thinkers, to require that the logically possible is radically distinct from the really possible. Craig points out that many mathematicians are willing to talk about the abstract possibility of infinite sets but shy away from the belief that these ideas could ever find application in the real world.[5] It may be that no logical inconsistency is involved in the notion of an infinite set but that there could never be, in the world of space and time, an infinite set of objects (existing either simultaneously or successively). If this were true, not only would the ontological argument be affected, the cosmological argument would suffer as well. For Hartshorne, existence (God's included) is essentially temporal. If Craig's contention is correct then the past cannot be infinite. Thus, if God exists then he is capable of existence without time. Although Hartshorne's arguments against the idea of timeless existence are, to my mind, convincing, Craig's point of view cannot be dismissed lightly. As noted in chapter V, Hartshorne admits that he is perplexed by the idea of the actual infinite.

Another point at which the global argument requires further support is in the doctrine that becoming is ontologically more basic than being. The design argument is founded on the principle that the natural order is the supreme instance of social order. Not everyone is comfortable with this panpsychist view of reality. Although I cannot count myself among their number—panpsychism always seemed to me to be too beautiful to be false—it is understandable why so many have rejected it. Although the objection is not decisive, panpsychism has never fared well with common sense.[6] On a more serious level, the social view of reality occasions several objections, not least of which is how the language describing human activity can legitimately be extended so as to encompass nonhuman modes of becoming. One way of putting the objection is to ask of what use even the most extended psychology can be to physics. These are difficult questions whose answers require more than the cursory treatment given them in chapter VI.

One of the most interesting challenges to Hartshorne's global argument arises from the allegation that neoclassical theism is incompatible with current physics. The charge is particularly interesting in light of the fact that Hartshorne has continuously waged war against the idea that God's existence is an empirical question. Of all of the challenges to the global argument this is the most potentially damaging since it threatens not only the argument for God's existence but the entire metaphysical enterprise as Hartshorne defines it. It behoves us to look at the problem in more detail.

Process philosophers have, for some time, been aware of the problems relativity physics poses for God, as neoclassically conceived.[7] According to recent physics, there is no absolute meaning to simultaneity. If A is simultaneous with B and B is simultaneous with C, it does not necessarily follow that A is simultaneous with C. The simultaneity relation is not transitive. The meaning of simultaneity (and thus, time) is always fixed by reference to some co-ordinate system. Thus, contrary to the Newtonian picture of time as an absolute frame of reference in terms of which an event can be located, Einsteinian physics teaches a relativistic theory of time. As Einstein says,

> Every reference body (co-ordinate system) has its own particular time; unless we are told the reference-body to which the statement of time refers, there is no meaning in a statement of the time of an event.[8]

The consequence of this view is that from one reference frame, x, two events, A and B, may be successive, while from another reference frame, y, A and B may be simultaneous. Since there is no meaning to time independent of a reference frame, the question whether A and B are *really* simultaneous has no meaning.

Several interrelated problems for neoclassical theism are occasioned by Einstein's views. According to Hartshorne, God is a temporal being. Does this not mean that God is subject to the same temporal limitations as other things? God is not, of course, subject to birth or death. But if, like other beings, he exists in time, then some meaning must be given to the concept of divine temporality. Relativity physics does not appear to permit us to fix the meaning of the divine time apart from some frame of reference within the space-time continuum. One hypothesis is that God occupies some privileged frame of reference within the world which enables him to know which events are really simultaneous and which are not. This hypothesis is contrary to Einstein's teaching that there is no meaning to the question of which events are really simultaneous. The hypothesis also seems to compromise the concept of God's omnipresence. But if we allow that God is present in every co-ordinate system then the concept of God's individuality becomes problematic. As Hartshorne says,

> If God *here now* is not the same concrete unit of reality as God somewhere else 'now', then the simple analogy with human

consciousness as a single linear succession of states collapses. (CS 124).

The answer that is given to these questions is going to involve a more complex view of God (or relativity physics) than we now have.

A variation on the problem of God's individuality is the problem of how the concept of "God's time" can be given meaning. Hartshorne does an admirable job of stating this objection.

> . . . there seems no way to divide the cosmic process as a whole into past and future. Yet if neoclassical theism is right, it seems there must, for God at least, be a way. What is God's 'frame of reference', if there is no objectively right frame of reference for the cut between past and future? (NT 93).

If there is something like a divine time, then it is not the time of relativity theory. God's past and future would not be a time that is available for the physicist to study.

I have purposefully avoided going into great detail describing the encounter of relativity physics with neoclassical theism. We are not so much interested in the ways some philosophers have tried to demonstrate the compatibility of physics and process theism as with the fact that such a controversy could ever arise. According to Hartshorne, metaphysical questions are completely a priori. No amount of empirical investigation can ever answer a truly metaphysical question. The reason for this is that metaphysics, according to Hartshorne, deals with the most general features of reality. The metaphysician is not so much concerned with what is true in the actual world as with what is true in any possible world. Yet, if this is true, and if the theistic question is, as Hartshorne maintains, metaphysical, then there should never have been any question about whether relativity physics is compatible with neoclassical theism. If relativity physics conflicts with theism then so does every other conceivable cosmological theory.

Hartshorne recognizes this difficulty and suggests that the conflict between his theism and relativity physics is only apparent.

> Unless some sort of physical relativity is compatible with deity, theism cannot even be logically possible—such would be my guess as to the logic of the matter. In that case, the observational facts are wholly neutral, as I hold they really must be. (NT 94).

The question, says Hartshorne, is whether physics can be expected to "give us the deep truth about time as it would appear to a non-localized observer." (CS 125). If Hartshorne is to be true to his metaphysical principles he must deny that physics has the final word.

Despite his insistence on the independence of physics and metaphysics, Hartshorne takes the findings of physics quite seriously. The most recent developments in the debate over relativity theory and Hartshorne's concept of God bear this out. Basing his theory on the work in quantum physics of J. S. Bell, Henry P. Stapp argues for a revised view of space-time according to which events may influence each other even though there is not enough time for a light signal to pass between them. The symmetrical independence of contemporaries taught by relativity theory would, then, have to be qualified.[9] The importance of this view, as Hartshorne sees, is to dissolve the problem of showing a compatibility between divine time and the time of which relativity theory speaks. There is only one world-line and this world-line can be identified with God's temporal reference frame, even if, for the purposes of relativity theory, such a world-line is not available to any localized observer. Hartshorne expresses relief at having had the philosophical burden of relativity physics lifted from his shoulders.

> For decades I have suffered philosophically from [the seeming necessity that contemporaries are mutually independent].
> Now, may Allah bless him, Bell has done away, it seems, with the problem.[10]

Not everyone agrees that the challenges to neoclassical theism from physics are dispelled by Stapp's arguments. The assumptions upon which Stapp founds his theory are themselves problematic.[11] The question of the relationship between Hartshorne's theism and relativity physics is still open.

The tantalizing question remains: If physics and metaphysics are, as Hartshorne maintains, autonomous disciplines, why is there an apparent conflict between relativity theory and neoclassical theism? The eagerness with which Hartshorne embraces Stapp's views as freeing neoclassical theism from the bonds of relativity theory does not square well with the claim that empirical issues can have no relevance for settling metaphysical problems. The very idea that a theory in physics could either pose a threat to, or vindicate, Hartshorne's theism suggests that there is a more intimate relationship between metaphysics and the empirical sciences than Hartshorne is willing to allow. It is this possibility which we must now explore.

Since metaphysics deals with what is true in every possible world, it is appropriate to call metaphysical issues conceptual. Furthermore, since a metaphysical truth could not, in any genuinely conceivable state of affairs, be false, metaphysical truths must be, as Hartshorne maintains, independent of anything that could be found by an empirical investigation. The problem arises when we try to give content to the notion of independence. Conceptual issues are never so well defined as might be desired. Very often, what appears to be logically possible is shown to be logically impossible by a consideration of the empirical facts. The example used in chapter IV is a case in point. Willliam Rowe takes the possibility of the existence of an eternal star as a counter-example to the claim that an eternal being cannot be contingent. The empirical facts about the internal composition and structure of stars, however, show that Rowe's claim is dubious. Rowe's eternal star could have none of the essential characteristics of stars as we know them. Thus, even if we were to discover something that had some of the superficial features of stars—for example, lighting up the night sky—but shared none of the essential features of stars, the thing we had discovered would not be a star. Thus, it is not clear that an eternal star is a star at all.

Other examples of the mutual relevance of empirical science and metaphysics are available. Although in this work, we have taken a stand against the traditional doctrine of creation *ex nihilo*, the problem of the world's creation provides an excellent example of how empirical and conceptual issues can dovetail. Kant objected to the idea that time began with the creation of the world on the grounds that it is always possible to imagine a moment before the creation of the world. There are, of course, purely philosophical answers to this position.[12] But discoveries in physics are also relevant to refuting Kant's argument. According to current cosmology, time and space are a function of the density of matter. The more dense matter becomes, the more contracted space and time become. If, as some scientists believe, the universe, as we know it, began from a state of infinite density, then space and time would have been infinitely contracted. Thus, prior to the "big bang" there would be no time as we understand the word.

> . . . the universe began from a state of infinite density . . .
> Space and time were created in that event and so was all the
> matter in the universe. It is not meaningful to ask what
> happened before the big bang; it is somewhat like asking what
> is north of the North Pole.[13]

Thus, Kant's conceptual objection to the idea of a beginning of time is refuted by current cosmological theory. This is not to say that *all* objections to the doctrine of creation *ex nihilo* are shown to be false. But Kant's argument surely cannot be taken as conclusive in light of the empirical evidence.

The discoveries made in the empirical sciences are not irrelevant to metaphysical issues. The important question this raises for Hartshorne's position is whether the existence of God is, after all, an empirical question. Let us suppose, for example, that physicists came to adopt the views of Lawrence Sklar who, by interpreting Minkowski spacetime in a literalistic way, asserts that future events "have determinate reality" and that future objects are "real existents."[14] Were this view to become the dominant trend in physics, it would constitute a formidable barrier to Hartshorne's philosophy according to which the future is partly indeterminate, even for God. Hartshorne is clear that his views on the nature of creativity lead him to reject any interpretation of relativity theory which would deny the reality of becoming (CS 125). My own beliefs about the possibility of freedom lead me to side with Hartshorne on this issue.[15] The point, however, is that what we believe about such fundamental concepts as time, space, cause, deity, etc., is profoundly influenced by the findings of the empirical sciences. The philosopher cannot ignore the findings of scientists, especially those findings which become well entrenched in scientific theories.

Despite the fact that empirical discoveries seem to have a bearing on metaphysical problems, it would be hasty to conclude that God's existence is an empirical question. The discoveries of empirical science may be relevant to metaphysical questions without being able to settle those questions.

We have already touched on the problem of creation *ex nihilo*. Modern physics demonstrates that the Kantian argument against a beginning of time is inconclusive. Nevertheless, physicists have not proved that there was ever a 'time' when the universe did not exist. Temporality, as it is available to physics, may have begun with the big bang. The qualification "as it is available to physics" is important. If there is, as Hartshorne claims, a divine time, there is no necessity that it should be available to physicists. Indeed, considerations internal to physics might suggest this conclusion. Some scientists believe that there might have been more than one big bang explosion in the past.[16] If this is so, and if the big bang marks the beginning of a universe's time, then time must have had several beginnings. The 'divine time' might, then, be the only measure of the sequence of universes. These considerations are admittedly speculative. The important thing is that they do not exceed the bounds of what it is reasonable to believe is really possible. Science, therefore, does not answer the question of creation *ex nihilo*, although it may shed light on the problem.

Similarly, science is not irrelevant to the quesiton of divine existence. Neoclassical theism's encounter with relativity physics is enough to prove this much. But to claim that science might prove or disprove the existence of God is going too far. I agree with Hartshorne that the question of God's existence is *a priori*. Anselm's ontological argument stands as a reminder of the inadequacy of any merely empirical approach to God's existence. One must distinguish, however, the bare fact (if it is a fact) that God exists and the particular manner in which we conceive of that existence. A particular concept of God may be shown to be inconsistent with empirically discoverable facts. This is not a proof that God does not exist. It is only proof that one conception of the divine existence is inadequate.

It should be noted that the distinction between God's existence and our concepts of God is not the same distinction as Hartshorne draws between God's existence and actuality. The existence/actuality distinction is part of Hartshorne's *concept* of God. But there are other concepts of God. One may argue that Hartshorne's concept of God is the most consistent, religiously adequate, etc., while recognizing that there are other candidates for these honors.

It is to the credit of some philosophers that they have insisted on making the distinction between our concepts of God and God's existence. A maze of confusion arises from conflating this distinction. For example, Flew's *God and Philosophy* is a sustained attack on God as classically conceived. In disposing of the classical concept of God, however, Flew believed himself to have proved more than what his arguments actually showed. He concluded to the nonexistence of God. He should have concluded only to the nonexistence of God as classically conceived.[17]

Some forms of the problem of evil also provide good examples of the danger of conflating the distinction between our concepts of God and God's existence. We are told, for example, that there is no good reason to believe that God exists since God would not allow children to die of terrible diseases. A response to this argument, that is too often ignored, is that the God whose existence these facts disprove is not the only God that is conceivable. We have seen in chapter VI that Hartshorne's concept of God does not entail that God prevents (or could prevent) every occurrence of moral or natural evil. There-fore, it does not follow from the inadequacy of any particular concept of God that there are no adequate conceptions of the divine existence.

My position, therefore, is that Hartshorne is correct in his belief that the existence of God is not an empirical question; but that he is wrong in thinking that science cannot discredit a particular concept of God, his own included. This is not to say that I believe science has discredited neoclassical theism. With some qualifications—some of which I have introduced in the course of the present work—Harts-horne's concept of God is the only form of theism I can accept. From my layman's knowledge, no one has conclusively shown that either relativity theory or quantum mechanics is incompatible with neo-classical theism. Nevertheless, such an incompatibility is possible. In that case, neoclassicism would either have to be revised or abandoned in favor of some other, as yet unimagined, form of theism. The problem is that any claim that such-and-such is genuinely conceivable cannot be divorced from empirical considerations. Scientific discoveries may lead us to believe that what we thought was conceivable is, in fact, a meaningless conjunction of concepts. Thus, it is the task of every theist who is concerned that his or her view of God is (more or less) correct, to show that the concept of God in question is compatible with the facts unearthed by science.

Hartshorne says that the only God with whom empirically discov-erable facts could be incompatible is an idol or a fetish (CS 30). In this, I agree with Hartshorne. The relation between science and meta-physics for which I have argued suggests that one task of science is to aid the metaphysician in unmaking idolotrous concepts of God. More generally, the importance of science for metaphysics is that we do not know *a priori*, where empirical questions end and where conceptual questions begin. As already noted, a concept may appear to be gen-uinely conceivable but on closer inspection be shown to harbor an inconsistency.

Much has been said about the relevance of science for metaphysics; but it is equally true that metaphysics has relevance for science. We have already seen a possible example of this in the concept of divine time as being the measure of time between big bangs. Hartshorne suggests another example when he says that relativity is not completely an empirical issue.

> Einstein's formula could be falsified; but the degree of relativity is one thing, the question of relativity or no relativity is another. (CS 124).

Thus, metaphysics may have important things to say to physicists about physics. This is precisely the situation one would expect if empirical and conceptual issues are not always clearly distinguishable.

An objection to the position for which I have argued is that it makes the falsification of the hypothesis that God exists impossible. If one can believe that God exists no matter what science discovers then it appears that the existence of God is not really an issue for rational discourse but, rather, a matter of blind faith. The problem with this objection is that it makes it appear as though the theist can never be under a rational complusion to abandon belief in God. But this is not a consequence of the view that empirical science cannot disprove the existence of God. There are other considerations, besides empirical science, relevant to evaluating the concept of God. If one became convinced, for example, that there is a contradiction in the very concept of a logically necessary being one might decide not to believe in God. In other words, one might come to the conclusion that there are no legitimate concepts of God nor that there are likely to be any. In this case, one would be denying not only that a particular concept of God is not instantiated but that God does not exist, that is, no concept of God worthy of consideration *could be* instantiated. If a theist became an atheist for this reason, the conversion might be regarded as a failure of faith by other theists. This fact simply demonstrates that a decision can be both rational and a failure of faith. It is by no means obvious that the requirements of faith are also the requirements of rationality. Pascal's statement that "the heart has its reasons which reason does not know" is too little appreciated in current discussions of philosophy of religion.[18]

Ideally, faith should be supplemented by a rational account. The proofs for God's existence are an attempt to provide such an account. To the extent that they are successful, reason is the ally of faith. Success is measured by a variety of factors including the consistency of the concept of God, the validity and soundness of the arguments, the degree to which the God that is being proved resembles God as understood by the religious community, and compatibility with the scientifically discovered facts. The scope of the present work has prohibited an extensive discussion of the empirical issues. Also, except for a few remarks, in chapter III, scant attention has been paid to the question of whether neoclassical theism captures the essential things religious people believe about God. On both of these issues let me simply register my opinion that I am optimistic that neither will produce serious objections to Hartshorne's theism. We have focused primarily on the questions of consistency, validity and soundness. Again, the verdict is positive. The major weakness of the global argument is the insufficient attention paid to the empirical issues. Contrary to Hartshorne's belief, his theism is not above a reproach based on the findings of science. I have argued that this fact does not make the existence of God an empirical question. Scientific discoveries can only lead to the revision of one's concept of God.

Notes

Introduction

[1]Charles Hartshorne, Forward to *The Ontological Argument of Charles Hartshorne* by George L. Goodwin (Missoula, Montana: Scholar's Press, 1978), p. xi.

[2]David A. Pailin, "Some Comments on Hartshorne's Presentation of the Ontological Argument," *Religious Studies*, 4, 1 (1968), p. 114.

[3]Charles Hartshorne, "What the Ontological Proof Does Not Do," *Review of Metaphysics*, 17, 4 (June 1964), pp. 608–609.

[4]The global argument was published in *The Monist*, 54, 2 (April 1970), pp. 159–180 and as Chapter XIV of CS.

[5]In a letter dated February 2, 1981 Hartshorne writes, "The account of the arguments in *Creative Synth*. [sic] is very brief and, I now think, is one reason it has had so little attention."

[6]Hartshorne's latest book, OT adopt the convention of referring to God by both feminine and masculine pronouns linked by a dash, for example, "He-She," "Him-Herself."

[7]Mary Daly, *Gyn/Ecology The Metaethics of Radical Feminism* (Boston: Beacon Press, 1978), p. xi.

[8]Rosemary Radford Reuther, "Motherearth and the Megamachine," in *Womanspirit Rising, A Feminist Reader in Religion*, edited by Carol P. Christ and Judith Plaskow (San Francisco: Harper & Row, 1979), pp. 43–52.

[9]Mary Daly, *Beyond God the Father Toward A Philosophy of Women's Liberation* (Boston: Beacon Press, 1973), p. 188.

Chapter I

[1]Basil Mitchell, *The Justification of Religious Belief* (New York: Seabury Press, 1973).

[2]Ibid., pp. 39–40.

[3]Ibid., p. 40.

[4]David Hume, *Dialogues Concerning Natural Religion*, Norman Kemp Smith, ed. (Indianapolis: Bobbs-Merrill, 1947).

[5]From the University Discussion on Theology and Falsification, in Antony Flew and Alasdair MacIntyre, eds., *New Essays in Philosophical Theology* (New York: Macmillan, 1955), p. 103.

[6]Mitchell, *The Justification of Religious Belief*, p. 45.

[7]See, for example, BH.

[8]Mitchell, *The Justification of Religious Belief*, p. 41–42.

[9]J. L. Mackie, *The Miracle of Theism, Arguments for and against the Existence of God* (Oxford: Clarendon Press, 1982), pp. 6–7.

[10]John Duns Scotus, *A Treatise on God as First Principle*, Allan B. Wolter, trans. (Chicago: Forum Books, 1966); F. R. Tennant, *Philosophical Theology*, vol. II (Cambridge: Cambridge University Press, 1930); David Elton Trueblood, *Philosophy of Religion*, (New York: Harper and Row, 1957).

[11]Frederick Copleston, *On the History of Philosophy* (New York: Barnes & Noble, 1979), p. 88.

[12]Trueblood, *Philosophy of Religion*, p. 74.

[13]Tennant, *Philosophical Theology*, p. 78.

[14]Trueblood, *Philosophy of Religion*, p. 81.

[15]Richard Swinburne, *The Existence of God* (Oxford: Clarendon Press, 1979).

[16]Ibid., p. 10.

[17]Antony Flew, *God and Philosophy* (London: Hutchinson, 1966); Michael Scriven, *Primary Philosophy* (New York: McGraw Hill, 1966); Alasdair MacIntyre, *Difficulties in Christian Belief* (New York: Philosophical Library, 1959).

[18]MacIntyre, *Difficulties in Christian Belief*, p. 63.

[19]Flew, *God and Philosophy*, p. 62.

[20]Mitchell, *The Justification of Religious Belief*, p. 160.

[21]Swinburne, *The Existence of God*, p. 13.

[22]Ibid.

[23]Flew, *God and Philosophy*, p. 141.

[24]Scriven, *Primary Philosophy*, p. 153.

[25]MacIntyre, *Difficulties in Christian Belief*, pp. 78–79.

[26]I am indebted to Dr. Kenneth Merrill for this last point.

[27]This argument was suggested to me by Ben Gary Nowlin.

[28]Alvin Plantinga, *The Nature of Necessity* (Oxford: Clarendon Press, 1974), p. 5.

[29]William James, *The Varieties of Religious Experience* (New York: Modern Library, 1929), p. 427.

Chapter II

[1]William Lad Sessions, "Hartshorne's Early Philosophy," in *Two Process Philosophers, Hartshorne's Encounter with Whitehead*, Lewis S. Ford, ed. (Tallashassee, Florida: American Academy of Religion, 1973), p. 29.

[2]OD, page 1 of the digest of the dissertation.

[3]Ibid.

[4]Sessions, "Hartshorne's Early Philosophy," p. 29.

[5]Ibid., p. 31.

[6]Charles Hartshorne, "James's Empirical Pragmatism," *American Journal of Theology and Philosophy*, 1, 1 (Jan. 1980), p. 17.

[7]For a more extensive discussion of the concepts of abstractness and concreteness in Hartshorne's dissertation see Sessions' "Hartshorne's Early Philosophy," pp. 30–31.

Chapter III

[1]See especially, MVG, Chapter I and CS, Chapter XIII.

[2]Thomas Aquinas, *On the Truth of the Catholic Faith, Book One: God*, a translation of *Summa Contra Gentiles* by Anton C. Pegis (Garden City, New York: Image, 1955), p. 101, 16.5.

[3]Frederick Copleston, *A History of Philosophy*, vol. 2 Part II (Garden City, New York: Image, 1962), p. 51.

[4]Aquinas, *Summa Contra Gentiles*, p. 103, 18.2.

[5]Copleston, *A History of Philosophy*, p. 250.

⁶Aquinas finds scriptual support for the doctrine of divine immutability in Malachi 3.6, James 1.17, and Numbers 23.19. See *Summa Contra Gentiles*, p. 97, 14.4.

⁷This is an analogy used by Aquinas, *Summa Contra Gentiles*, p. 219, 66.7.

⁸Aquinas, *Summa Contra Gentiles*, p. 218, 66.6.

⁹For an excellent review of traditional theodicies see David Ray Griffin's *God, Power, and Evil: A Process Theodicy* (Philadelphia: Westminster Press, 1976).

¹⁰Edward Madden and Peter Hare, *Evil and the Concept of God* (Springfield, Illinois: Charles C. Thomas Pub., 1968), pp. 115–125.

¹¹Charles Hartshorne, "The Dipolar Conception of Deity," *Review of Metaphysics*, 21, 2 (Dec. 1967), p. 283.

¹²Charles Hartshorne, "A New Look at the Problem of Evil," in *Current Philosophical Issues: Essays in Honor of Curt John Ducasse*, compiled and edited by Frederick C. Pommeyer (Springfield, Illinois: Charles C. Thomas Pub., 1966), p. 203.

¹³This analysis provides the answer to Barry L. Whitney's question in his "Process Theism: Does a Persuasive God Coerce?" *Southern Journal of Philosophy*, 17, 1 (Spring 1979), pp. 133–143.

¹⁴Ibid., p. 206.

¹⁵Charles Hartshorne, "Taking Freedom Seriously," unpublished sermon delivered to the First Unitarian Church in Oklahoma City, Oklahoma, February 22, 1981.

¹⁶Hartshorne, "A New Look at the Problem of Evil," p. 206.

¹⁷John K. Roth, "A Theodicy of Protest," in *Encountering Evil, Live Options in Theodicy*, Steven T. Davis, editor (Atlanta, Georgia: John Knox Press, 1981), p. 13.

¹⁸J. L. Mackie, *The Miracle of Theism* (London: Oxford University Press, 1982), p. 176.

¹⁹Elsewhere Hartshorne emphasizes his faith in "the infallible wisdom and ideal power of God" in setting limits to the freedom in the universe. But, he adds, "if I play at criticizing God it is at this point." (OT 126).

²⁰Charles Hartshorne, Replys to questions in *Philosophical Interrogations*, Sydney and Beatrice Rome, eds. (New York: Holt, Rinehart and Winston, 1964), p. 343.

²¹Charles Hartshorne, "Could There Have Been Nothing? A Reply [to Craighead]," *Process Studies* 1, 1 (Spring 1971), pp. 25–28.

²²The classic statement of this view can be found in Bonaventure's *The Mind's Road to God*, trans. and with an introduction by George Boas (New York: Liberal Arts Press, 1953).

²³Bernardino M. Bonansea, *God and Atheism* (Washington, D.C.: The Catholic University Press of America, 1979), p. 164: John J. Shepherd, *Experience, Inference and God* (London: Macmillan, 1975), p. 118. Shepherd is particularly concerned that a contradiction is involved in calling God both necessary and contingent, cf. Chapter V, footnote 22 of this book.

²⁴Hartshorne also notes that there is a sense in which God is actually infinite. If the world has always existed, as Hartshorne believes, then there are an infinite number of past moments. In his inclusion of this infinite, God would also be actually infinite. (CS 235).

²⁵Aquinas, *Summa Contra Gentiles*, p. 100, 16.2.

²⁶Henry L. Ruf, "The Impossibility of Hartshorne's God," *Philosophical Forum* (Boston) 7, (1976), p. 349.

²⁷Ibid.

[28]Robert Neville, *Creativity and God: A Challenge to Process Theology* (New York: Seabury Press, 1980), p. 61.

[29]Charles Hartshorne, "Three Responses to Neville's *Creativity and God*," given by Charles Hartshorne, John B. Cobb, Jr., and Lewis S. Ford, *Process Studies*, 10, 3–4 (Winter 1980), p. 95.

[30]'Plenarism' comes from the Latin 'plenus', meaning 'full'. Plenarism is the opposite of nihilism. The doctrine of plenarism implies that there is a fullness to life akin to what Jesus meant by the abundant life (cf. John 10.10).

Chapter IV

[1]Charles Hartshorne, Foreword to *The Onological Argument of Charles Hartshorne* by George L. Goodwin (Missoula, Montana: Scholar's Press, 1978), p. xi.

[2]Ibid.

[3]David A. Pailin, "An Introductory Survey of Charles Hartshorne's Work on the Ontological Argument," in *Analecta Anselmiana*, volume 1, edited by F. S. Schmitt (Frankfurt-am-Maini: Minerya, 1969).

[4]Charles Hartshorne, "The Formal Validity and Real Significance of the Ontological Argument," *The Philosophical Review*, 53, 3 (May 1944), p. 236.

[5]Charles Hartshorne, "What the Ontological Proof Does Not Do," *Review of Metaphysics*, 17, 4 (June, 1964), p. 609.

[6]Charles Hartshorne, "John Hick on Logical and Ontological Necessity," *Religious Studies* 13, 2 (June 1977), p. 161.

[7]Norman Malcolm, "Anselm's Ontological Arguments." *The Philosophical Review* 69, 1 (January 1960), pp. 41–62. Hartshorne made the same point in 1953, see *PSG* 96–97. The point was made somewhat less clearly in "The Formal Validity and Real Significance of the Ontological Argument."

[8]See for example, J. Brenton Stearns, "Anselm and the Two Argument Hypothesis," *Monist* 54, 2 (April 1970), pp. 221–233, and Gregory Schufreider, *An Introduction to Anselm's Argument* (Philadelphia: Temple University Press, 1978).

[9]Hartshorne, "The Formal Validity and Real Significance of the Ontological Argument," p. 225.

[10]See the Foreword to this book (page ix), for this version of the argument. This is substantially the same form of the argument as given in *AD* 92. The major difference between the argument of *CS* and the argument considered in this chapter is that, in *CS*, the idea that deity is an "unactualizable ideal or limiting concept" is among the alternatives rejected. This view shares, with the atheistic view, the assumption that it is possible that the concept of God is coherent but that God does not exist. The following discussion of Anselm's principle, I think, discredits this assumption.

[11]Hartshorne, "Grounds For Believing in God's Existence," *Meaning, Truth, and God*, Leroy S. Rouner, ed., Boston University Studies in Philosophy and Religion, v. 3 (Notre Dame and London: University of Notre Dame Press, 1982), p. 21.

[12]R. L. Purtill, "Hartshorne's Modal Proof," *The Journal of Philosophy* 63, 14 (July 1966), pp. 397–409.

[13]Ibid., 398.

[14]Tomis Kapitan, "Perfection and Modality: Charles Hartshorne's Ontological Proof," *International Journal for the Philosophy of Religion* 7 (1976), p. 381.

[15]Anselm, *St. Anselm: Basic Writings* translated by S. N. Deane (La Salle, Illinois: Open Court, 1966), p. 8.

[16]Charles Hartshorne, Replys to questions in *Philosophical Interrogations*, Sydney and Beatrice Rome, eds. (New York: Holt, Rinehart and Winston, 1964), p. 347.

[17]Hick's articles include, "God as Necessary Being," *Journal of Philosophy* 57, 22 and 23 (November 1960), pp. 725–734: Review of Hartshorne's *The Logic of Perfection* in *Theology Today* 20, 2 (July 1963), pp. 295–298; "A Critique of the 'Second Argument'" in *The Many-Faced Argument*, edited by John Hick and Arthur C. McGill (New York: Macmillan, 1967), pp. 341–356; *Arguments for God's Existence* (New York: Seabury Press, 1971), Chapter 6.

[18]Hick, "A Critique of the 'Second Argument'," pp. 341–342.

[19]Hick, *Arguments for God's Existence*, p. 86.

[20]William Lycan, "Eternal Existence and Necessary Existence," *Notre Dame Journal of Formal Logic* 17, 2 (April 1976), pp. 287–290; Alvin Plantinga, "A Valid Ontological Argument?" in *The Ontological Argument*, edited by Alvin Plantinga (New York: Doubleday, 1965), pp. 160–171.

[21]Plantinga, "A Valid Ontological Argument?" p. 165.

[22]Charles Hartshorne, "Is the Denial of Existence Ever Contradictory," *Journal of Philosophy* 63, 4 (February 17, 1966), p. 89.

[23]Charles Hartshorne, "Real Possibility," *Journal of Philosophy* 61, 21 (October 10, 1963), p. 596.

[24]Personal letter dated May 4, 1981.

[25]Hartshorne, "John Hick on Logical and Ontological Necessity," p. 161.

[26]Anselm, *St. Anselm: Basic Writings*, pp. 150–151; Paul Henle, "Uses of the Ontological Argument," in the *The Ontological Argument*, Plantinga, ed., p. 173; William Rowe, *The Cosmological Argument* (Princeton: Princeton University Press, 1975), p. 52; Lycan, "Eternal Existence and Necessary Existence," p. 290.

[27]Rowe, *The Cosmological Argument*, p. 52.

[28]Alfred North Whitehead, *Process and Reality* corrected edition, David Ray Griffin and Donald Sherburne, eds. (New York: Free Press, 1978), p. 343.

[29]The argument here is independent of the issue of whether truth is eternal. For whether or not truth is eternal, there are contingent truths (unless one is a Spinozist). And if contingent matters are only causally intelligible, then Hartshorne has made his point.

[30]David Hume, *Dialogues Concerning Natural Religion*, Norman Kemp Smith, ed. (Indianapolis: Bobbs-Merrill Press, 1947), p. 189.

[31]Kai Neilsen, "Necessity and God," *International Journal for Philosophy of Religion*, volume 9 (1979), p. 18.

[32]Ibid.

[33]I am indebted to George Mavrodes for pointing this out to me.

[34]Ben Gary Nowlin, "The Ontological Argument: Sound But Superfluous?" unpublished manuscript; R. L. Purtill, "Ontological Modalities," *Review of Metaphysics* 21, 2 (December 1967), pp. 297–307.

[35]Nowlin, "The Ontological Argument: Sound But Superfluous?"

[36]Charles Hartshorne, "Rejoinder to Purtill," *Review of Metaphysics* 21, 2 (December 1967), p. 308.

[37]Michael Scriven, *Primary Philosophy* (New York: McGraw Hill, 1966), pp. 102–107.

[38]Hartshorne, "John Hick on Logical and Ontological Necessity," p. 156.

Chapter V

[1]See William L. Rowe, *The Cosmological Argument* (Princeton: Princeton University Press, 1975). For an interesting discussion on the idea that Aquinas' arguments are *a priori* see Louis Mackey, "Entreatments of God: Reflections on Aquinas' Five Ways," *Franciscan Studies* 37, Annual XV (1977), pp. 103–119.

[2]Since the argument of the dissertation is founded on the concept of Being, it is reasonable to call the argument cosmological. The ontological argument is founded on the concept of a perfect being. The perfection of existence, namely, necessary existence, is deduced from the concept of a perfect being.

[3]Houston Craighead, "Non-Being and Hartshorne's Concept of God," *Process Studies*, 1, 1 (Spring 1971), p. 14.

[4]Ibid.

[5]John Hick, "Theology and Verification," in *The Existence of God*, edited by John Hick (New York: Macmillan, 1964), p. 258.

[6]Ibid.

[7]Henri Bergson, *Creative Evolution*, Arthur Mitchell trans. (New York: Modern Library, 1944), pp. 304–305.

[8]For a discussion of this issue see William L. Reese, "Non-Being and Negative Reference," *Process and Divinity*, William L. Reese and Eugene Freeman, eds. (La Salle, Illinois: Open Court, 1964), pp. 311–323.

[9]William Lane Craig, *The Cosmological Argument from Plato to Leibniz* (New York: Barnes & Nobel, 1979), p. 52.

[10]For an excellent exposition of Bonaventure's arguments see Bernardino M. Bonansea, *God and Atheism* (Washington, D. C.: Catholic University Press, 1979), pp. 327–338.

[11]William Lane Craig, *The Kalam Cosmological Argument* (New York: Barnes & Nobel, 1979).

[12]Immanual Kant, *Critique of Pure Reason*, Norman Kemp Smith, trans. (London: Macmillan, 1929), p. 397.

[13]For other comments concerning God and the actual infinite see CS 126.

[14]Craig, *The Kalam Cosmological Argument*, p. 105.

[15]Bertrand Russell, *The Analysis of Mind* (London: George Allen & Unwin Ltd., 1921), pp. 159–160.

[16]Francis J. Kovach, "The Question of the Eternity of the World in St. Bonaventure and St. Thomas—A Critical Analysis," in *Bonaventure & Aquinas*, Robert Shahan and Francis J. Kovach, eds. (Norman: University of Oklahoma Press, 1976), p. 170.

[17]Craig, *The Kalam Cosmological Argument*. p. 69.

[18]I am indebted to Gary Nowlin for this point.

[19]Charles Hartshorne, "Negative Facts and the Analogical Inference to 'Other Mind'," *Dr. S. Radhakrishnan Souvenir Volume*. J. P. Atreya, ed. (Morabadad, India: Darshana Int., 1964), p. 149.

[20]An extensive discussion of current disputes surrounding *de re* modality can be found in Alvin Plantinga, *The Nature of Necessity* (Oxford: Clarendon Press, 1978), Chapters I, II, III.

[21]See Russell's debate with Copleston in Hick's *The Existence of God*, pp. 173–174.

²²John J. Shepherd, *Experience, Inference and God* (London: Macmillan, 1975), p. 24. It should be noted that the thrust of Shepherd's own position is to contrast the contingency of the universe with the divine necessary existence. According to Shepherd, "each of these logically excludes the other as a mode of existence of one and same being." (pp. 117–118). Shepherd believes his argument refutes Hartshorne's claim that God is necessarily dependent on some world or other. A necessary being, says Shepherd, is dependent on nothing external to its existence. I suspect Shepherd's argument rests on an ambiguity in the concept of dependence. God does not depend on the universe for his existence in the same sense that the universe depends upon God for its existence. Any particular universe depends upon the sustaining activity of God for its existence. God's existence, on the other hand, is dependent upon no particular state of affairs. Since Hartshorne believes that it is a necessary truth that something nondivine always exists, God's dependence on the universe is only the dependence of logical entailment. God's existence is not dependent on any particular universe that happens to exist but only on the abstract (and necessary) truth that there is a universe. Shepherd might reply by denying that something nondivine must exist. But as far as I can tell, Shepherd's arguments support no more than what Hartshorne affirms, namely, that no particular world exists of logical necessity.

²³Notice that the principle of contrast does not entail the claim that an entity must occupy only one pole of the contrast. Wittgenstein's point that something may be simple in relation to a certain whole and complex in relation to another does not argue against the validilty of the principle of contrast but only against a rather naive interpretation of it.

²⁴Brand Blanshard, "Reply to Charles Hartshorne," *The Philosophy of Brand Blanshard*, Paul A. Schilpp, ed. (La Salle, Illinois: Open Court, 1980), p. 642.

²⁵Plantinga, *The Nature of Necessity*, pp. 213–214.

²⁶"Ahriman, when the battle is over, is not destroyed as a substance—for a substance is by definition indestructible—but he is, to use the Pahlavī word a-kār-enīt, he is 'put out of action' or 'deprived of actuality': He is relegated to an eternal potency which can never be actualized again, or in more everyday language for people unfamiliar with the Aristotelian jargon, 'they drag Ahriman outside the sky and cut off his head'.", R. C. Zaehner, *The Teachings of the Magi* (London: Sheldon Press, 1975), p. 58.

Chapter VI

¹Plato's version of the argument is in *The Laws*, Book X. F. R. Tennant's "Cosmic Teleology" is in his *Philosophical Theology*, volume II (Cambridge: Cambridge University Press, 1928). Hartshorne would say that Plato's design argument is at least as sophisticated as Tennant's. (*IO* 35–39).

²Charles Hartshorne, "Can There Be Proofs for the Existence of God," in *Religious Language and Knowledge*, Robert H. Ayers and William T. Blackstone, eds. (Athens, Georgia: University of Georgia Press, 1972), pp. 62–75. "Grounds for Believing in God's Existence," *Meaning, Truth, and God*, edited by Leroy S. Rouner (Notre Dame and London: University of Notre Dame Press, 1982), pp. 18–20.

³Tennant, *Philosophical Theology*, p. 82. Richard Swinburne makes the same point, "The universe might so naturally have been chaotic, but it is not—it is very orderly," *The Existence of God* (Oxford: Clarendon Press, 1979), p. 136.

⁴C. S. Peirce, *Collected Papers of Charles Sanders Peirce*, volume V, Charles Hartshorne and Paul Weiss, eds. (Cambridge: Harvard University Press, 1934), p. 152.

⁵Michael Scriven, *Primary Philosophy* (New York: McGraw Hill, 1966), p. 126.

⁶Charles Hartshorne, "Paul Weiss's *The God We Seek*," *Review of Metaphysics* 25, Supplement (June 1972), p. 112.

⁷A. N. Whitehead, *Process and Reality*, corrected edition, Donald Sherburne and David Ray Griffin, eds. (New York: Free Press, 1978), p. 21.

⁸Ibid.

⁹Charles Hartshorne, Replies to questions in *Philosophical Interrogations*, Sydney and Beatrice Rome, eds. (New York: Holt, Rinehart Winston, 1964), p. 321.

¹⁰Charles Hartshrone, "Theism in Asian and Western Thought," *Philosophy East and West* 28, 4 (October 1978), p. 407.

¹¹J. L. Mackie, *The Miracle of Theism* (Oxford: Clarendon Press, 1982), pp. 150—176; H. J. McCloskey, "God and Evil," *God and Evil* edited by Nelson Pike (Englewood Cliffs, N.J.: Prentice-Hall, 1964). Antony Flew, "Divine Omnipotence and Human Freedom," in *New Essays in Philosophical Theology*, Antony Flew and Alasdair MacIntyre, eds. (New York: Macmillan, 1955), pp. 144—169. Edward Madden and Peter Hare, *Evil and the Concept of God*, (Springfield, Illinois: Charles C. Thomas Pub., 1968). Peter Hutcheson, unpublished personal correspondence.

¹²(For a more thorough rebuttal of Flew's argument see Frederick Ferre), *Language, Logic and God* (New York: Harper and Row, 1961), pp. 116—120.

¹³Donald Wayne Viney, *Freedom and Responsibility: A Whiteheadian Perspective*, unpublished Master's Thesis, University of Oklahoma,1979, Chapter II.

¹⁴Charles Hartshorne, "The God of Religion and the God of Philosophy," *Talk of God*, Royal Institute of Philosophy Lectures, Volume 2, 1967–1968 (New York: Macmillan, 1969), p. 160.

¹⁵Charles Hartshorne, "A Philosophy of Death," in *Philosophical Aspects of Thanatology*, volume II, M. Florence and A. H. Kutscher, eds. (New York: MSS Information Corporation, 1978), p. 87.

¹⁶Ralph Waldo Emerson, "Compensation," *Emerson's Essays* (New York: Houghton Mifflin Co., 1876), p. 99.

¹⁷Hartshorne, "A Philosophy of Death," p. 86.

¹⁸Charles Hartshorne, "The Dipolar Conception of Deity," *Review of Metaphysics* 21, 2 (December, 1967), p. 284.

¹⁹I am indebted to a conversation with Gary Nowlin for this point.

²⁰Alvin Plantinga, "The Probability Argument from Evil," *Philosophical Studies* 35, 1 (January 1979), pp. 1–54.

²¹Charles Hartshorne, "What Did Anselm Discover?" *Union Seminary Quarterly Review*, 17 (1962), pp. 213–222. This paper appears as Chapter 8 of *IO*.

Chapter VII

¹Charles Hartshorne, "Ideal Knowledge Defines Reality: What was True in 'Idealism'," *The Journal of Philosophy* 43, 21 (Oct. 10, 1946), pp. 573–582 (hereafter referred to as IK); see also p. 724 of the same volume for a correction; PSG 146–148, 197–198, 206–208; "Royce and the Collapse of Idealism," *Revue Internationale de Philosophie* 23 (1967), pp. 46–59 (hereafter referred to as RI).

[2]We do not mean to imply that the distinction between phenomena and noumena is the same as the distinction between appearance and reality for Kant. Even within the phenomenal world a distinction has to be maintained between appearance and reality. Kant uses the traditional distinction between primary and secondary qualities toward this end.

[3]RI, p. 50.

[4]Tarski says, " . . . we may accept the semantic conception of truth without giving up any epistemological attitude we may have had; we may remain naive realists, critical realists or idealists, empiricists or metaphysicians—whatever we were before. The semantic conception is completely neutral toward all these issues." Alfred Tarski, "The Semantic Conception of Truth and the Foundations of Semantics," *Philosophy and Phenomenological Research* 4 (1944), p. 362.

[5]RI, p. 52.

[6]Charles Hartshorne, "The Dipolar Conception of Deity," *The Review of Metaphysics* 21, 2 (Dec. 1967), p. 277.

[7]Charles Hartshorne, "Paul Weiss's The God We Seek," *The Review of Metaphysics* 25, Supplement (June 1972), p. 111.

[8]Ibid.

[9]IK, p. 578.

[10]The atheist might wish to claim that the possibly existing ideal knower need not be God. Yet, even if this is possible—which I deny—it is still true that the ideal knower could not know his own nonexistence.

[11]IK, p. 581.

[12]IK, p. 575.

[13]Gary Nowlin, *The Reasonableness of Faith as a Response to Evil*, unpublished dissertation, University of Oklahoma, 1981, p. 1. Hartshorne discusses Ross's theodicy in CS 242.

[14]IK, p. 577.

[15]Charles Hartshorne, Personal letter, dated February 21, 1982.

Chapter VIII

[1]Immanuel Kant, *Critique of Practical Reason*, Lewis White Beck, trans. (New York: Bobbs-Merrill, 1956), pp. 126–136.

[2]William James suggests a form of the moral argument (following Royce) in *The Will to Believe and Other Essays in Popular Philosophy* (New York: Dover Publications, Inc., 1956, originally published by Longmans, Green & Co., 1897), pp. 213–214; other well-known defenders of the argument include Hastings Rashdall, *The Theory of Good and Evil*, volume II (Oxford: Clarendon Press, 1907), pp. 205–213; W. R. Sorley, *Moral Values and the Idea of God* (London: Cambridge University Press, 1924), Chapter XIII; F. R. Tennant, *Philosophical Theology*, Volume II (London: Cambridge University Press, 1930), pp. 93–99; and most recently, Robert Merrihew Adams has revived the divine command theory of morality, "A Modified Divine Command Theory of Ethical Wrongness," in *Religion and Morality*, Gene Outka and John P. Reeder, eds. (Garden City, New York: Doubleday, 1973), pp. 318–347.

[3]After delivering a sermon at the First Unitarian Church in Oklahoma City on February 22, 1981, Hartshorne was asked, "Why bother with God?" Hartshorne replied with his moral argument. In April 1983 Hartshorne told me in private con-

versation that the two arguments of the global argument he finds most compelling are the design and moral arguments.

⁴Charles Hartshorne, "Ethics and the New Theology," *International Journal of Ethics* 45, 1 (October 1934), pp. 90–101.

⁵Charles Hartshorne, "Can There Be Proofs for the Existence of God?" in *Religious Language and Knowledge*, Robert H. Ayers and William T. Blackstone, eds. (Athens, Georgia: University of Georgia Press, 1972), pp. 62–75; "Grounds for Believing in God's Existence," in *Meaning, Truth, and God*, Leroy S. Rouner, ed. (Notre Dame and London: University of Notre Dame Press, 1982), pp. 26–28.

⁶Hartshorne, "Can There Be Proofs for the Existence of God?", p. 72.

⁷Ibid., p. 73.

⁸Edward Westermarck, *Ethical Relativity* (London: Kegan Paul, Trench, Trubner & Company, 1932).

⁹Tennant, *Philosophical Theology*, p. 98.

¹⁰Bertrand Russell, *Why I Am Not A Christian* (New York: Simon and Schuster, 1957), p. 6.

¹¹Ibid., p. 107.

¹²Charles Hartshorne, "Theism in Asian and Western Thought," *Philosophy East and West* 28, 4 (October 1978), p. 410.

¹³Hartshorne, "Can There Be Proofs for the Existence of God?", p. 70.

¹⁴Jorge Luis Borges, *Dreamtigers* (Austin, Texas: University of Texas Press, 1964), p. 39.

¹⁵I am indebted to my wife, Chris, for this argument. It might be claimed that the second law of thermodynamics, when applied to the universe as a whole supports Hartshorne's argument. The problem is that the second law applies only to closed systems and it it is not clear that the universe counts as a closed system. Again, I have Chris to thank for pointing this out to me.

¹⁶Hartshorne, "Can There Be Proofs for the Existence of God?", p. 70.

¹⁷Ibid., p. 71.

¹⁸C. S. Lewis, *The Problem of Pain* (New York: Macmillan, 1959, originally published 1940), pp. 103–104. Hartshorne quotes this passage in "Philosophy and Orthodoxy," *Ethics* 54, 4 (July 1944), p. 296. Antony Flew also deals with this passage in "Divine Omnipotence and Human Freedom," *New Essays in Philosophical Theology*, Antony Flew and Alasdair MacIntyre, eds. (New York: Macmillan, 1955), p. 148. Flew refuses to face the Hartshornean problem by simply labeling it a "truism" that more suffering is worse, all else being equal.

¹⁹Flew says it is "monstrous" for Lewis to imply that more people being in pain "makes no value difference." "Divine Omnipotence and Human Freedom," p. 148. I fail to see that Lewis has implied anything of this sort.

²⁰That the problem of a multiplicity of beneficiaries does not arise for individuals is especially apparent when the individual is God. Hartshorne would say that God is the only individual for whom the multiplicity of beneficiaries could not be a problem since God is the only individual who could enjoy infalliable recall of all past moments of his life.

²¹Lewis S. Ford and Marjorie Suckocki, "A Whiteheadian Reflection on Immortality," in *Philosophical Aspects of Thanatology*, volume II, Florence M. Hetzler and A. H. Kutscher, eds. (New York: MSS Information Corporation, 1978), pp. 67–79.

[22]John Hick, who believes in immortality, concedes this point but says that through numerous deaths the unity of the individual might be saved. It is not clear to me how this is supposed to solve the problem. See Hick's *Death and Eternal Life* (San Francisco: Harper & Row, 1976), pp. 413–414.

[23]Cebes, in Plato's *Phaedo* suggests this, 87b–88c.

[24]Hartshorne compares a person's life with a book in *LP* 250. I have taken the analogy in a direction of which Hartshorne might disapprove.

[25]Ninian Smart, "Omnipotence, Evil and Supermen," in *God and Evil*, Nelson Pike, ed. (Englewood Cliffs, N. J.: Prentice Hall, 1964), pp. 103–112. Hartshorne is also aware of the problem of applying ethical categories to God. See *CS* 309–310.

[26]Charles Hartshorne, "Philosophy After Fifty Years," in *Mid-Twentieth Century American Philosophy: Personal Statements*, Peter Bertocci, ed. (New York: Humanities Press, 1974), p. 149.

Chapter IX

[1]See *OD*, section 12, and *MVG*, chapter VI.

[2]Charles Hartshorne, *The Philosophy and Psychology of Sensation* (Port Washington, N.Y.: Kennikat Press, 1968; first published by University of Chicago Press, 1934); *Born to Sing, An Interpretation and World Survey of Bird Song* (Bloomington, Indiana: University of Indiana Press, 1973).

[3]A. J. Ayer, *Language, Truth and Logic* (New York: Dover Pub., 1946).

[4]See John Hosper's article in the *Encyclopedia of Philosophy*, Volume I, Paul Edwards, ed. (New York: Collier Macmillan, 1967), "Aesthetics, Problems of," pp. 52–55. For an elegant defense of subjectivism see Carlton Berenda's *World Visions and the Image of Man* (New York: Vantage Press, 1965).

[5]Hartshorne, *The Philosophy and Psychology of Sensation*, p. 94.

[6]For a detailed critique of this argument see Francis J. Kovach, "The Disagreement-Argument and Aesthetic Subjectivism," *The New Scholasticism*, 53, 1 (Winter 1979), pp. 22–41.

[7]Hartshorne, *The Philosophy and Psychology of Sensation*, p. 159.

[8]Hartshorne makes a similar point elsewhere, "All aesthetic value is either beauty or not too extreme deviation from it in one of the four directions: toward mere chaos or lifeless order; toward negligible complexity and intensity or baffling complexity, unattainable intensity." *Born to Sing*, p. 8.

[9]Charles Hartshorne, "Twelve Elements of My Philosophy," *The Southwestern Journal of Philosophy*, 5, 1 (Spring 1974), p. 12.

[10]C. S. Lewis, *Surprised by Joy* (New York: Harcourt Brace Jovanovich, 1955), p. 204.

[11]Charles Hartshorne, "Is God's Existence a State of Affairs?" in *Faith and the Philosophers*, edited by John Hick (New York: St. Martin's Press, 1964), p. 28.

Chapter X

[1]Hartshorne is careful to distinguish the capacity of a concept to individuate, from its capacity to particularize or concretize. A concept individuates an individual if the concept could not, in principle, refer to any other individual. 'Man' does not individuate Socrates since there are other men besides Socrates. A concept particularizes

an individual if it is capable of exhausting the qualitative aspects of the individual. According to Hartshorne, no concept is capable of particularizing an individual. The qualitative side of a person always contains more than could be expressed in any language. One is reminded of Whitehead's thought that mothers ponder many things in their hearts which their lips cannot express.

[2]Hartshorne seems to be in substantial agreement with the theory of reference developed by Kripke, Donnellan, Putnam, and others, see Steven P. Schwartz, ed., *Naming, Necessity and Natural Kinds* (Ithaca and London: Cornell University Press, 1977). Where Hartshorne would disagree with the new theory of reference is in the theory's apparent implication that *no* individual can be specified by concepts alone. Hartshorne would say that God is the one exception to this rule. Kripke seems to see this possibility when he wonders whether 'God' is a name or a description, cf. Saul A. Kripke, *Naming and Necessity* (Cambridge, Mass.: Harvard University Press, 1980), pp. 26–27.

[3]Charles Hartshorne, "Synthesis as Polydyadic Inclusion: A Reply to Sessions' 'Charles Hartshorne and Thirdness'," *Southern Journal of Philosophy* 14, 2 (Summer 1976), p. 247.

[4]John Duns Scotus, *Philosophical Writings*, Allan Wolter, trans. (Indianapolis: Bobbs-Merrill Pub., 1962), p. 94.

[5]William Lane Craig, *The Kalam Cosmological Argument* (New York: Barnes & Nobel, 1979), pp. 69–71.

[6]A good friend tells me he finds it difficult to present the idea of panpsychism to his classes without making it sound as though the world were composed of a bunch of smiley faces.

[7]John T. Wilcox, "A Question from Physics for Certain Theists," *Journal of Religion* 41, 1 (Oct. 1961), pp. 293–300.

[8]Albert Einstein, *Relativity* (New York: Crown Publ, 1961), p. 26

[9]Henry Peirce Stapp, "Quantum Mechanics, Local Causality, and Process Philosophy," edited by William B. Jones, *Process Studies* 7, 3 (Fall 1977), pp. 173–182.

[10]Charles Hartshorne, "Bell's Theorem and Stapp's Revised View of Space-Time," *Process Studies* 7, 3 (Fall 1977), p. 185.

[11]William B. Jones, "Bell's Theorem, H. P. Stapp, and Process Theism," *Process Studies* 7, 4 (Winter 1977), pp. 250–261.

[12]Thomas Aquinas argues that the time before the creation of the world is only an imaginary time. See *Summa Contra Gentiles*, Book II, Anton G. Pegis, trans. (New York: Image, 1955), 36, 1126.

[13]J. Richard Gott III, James E. Gunn, David N. Schramm, and Beatrice M. Tinsley, "Will the Universe Expand Forever?" *Scientific American* (March 1976), p. 65.

[14]Lawrence Sklar, *Space, Time and Spacetime* (Berkeley: University of California Press, 1974), p. 274. I am indebted to Craig's *The Kalam Cosmological Argument*, p. 107, for this phrasing.

[15]Donald Wayne Viney, *Freedom and Responsibility: A Whiteheadian Perspective*, unpublished Master's thesis, University of Oklahoma, 1979, chapter II.

[16]If the so-called oscillating model of the universe is true then there would be a series of big bang explosions. The issue, apparently still alive in physics, is whether the average density of the universe is great enough to cause the universe to collapse back on itself. For a discussion of this problem geared to the lay audience see Issac

Asimov, "The Very Large Lion and the Very Small Mouse," *Omni* (August 1981), pp. 79–83, 108.

[17]Schubert Ogden makes this point in his review of Flew's book, "God and Philosophy: A Discussion With Antony Flew," *Journal of Religion*, 48, 2 (April 1968), pp. 161–181.

[18]Blaise Pascal, *Pensées and the Provincial Letters*, translated by W. F. Trotter and Thomas M'Crie (New York: Modern Library, 1941), p. 95, number 277. An excellent discussion of the nature of faith is found in James L. Muyskens, *The Sufficiency of Hope (Philadelphia: Temple University Press, 1979)*.

Index of Persons

Subject Index